D1101971

Essential
Calculator Practice
for First Examinations

Peter Sherran BA
Woodhouse High School, Tamworth

Stanley Thornes (Publishers) Ltd

First published in 1986 by
Stanley Thornes (Publishers) Ltd
Old Station Drive
Leckhampton
CHELTENHAM GL53 0DN
England

British Library Cataloguing in Publication Data

Sherran, Peter
    Essential calculator practice for first
    examinations.
    1.   Calculators—Problems, exercises
    I.   Title
    510'.28 QA75

    ISBN   0–85950–618–5

Typeset by Tech-Set, Gateshead, Tyne & Wear in $9\frac{1}{2}/11\frac{1}{2}$ Century
Printed and bound in Great Britain by Ebenezer Baylis & Son, Worcester.

PREFACE

The aim of this book is to help pupils develop the necessary expertise to make efficient and effective use of an electronic calculator. It also aims to create an awareness that the results of any calculations must be checked and interpreted to ascertain that they are reasonable.

The preliminary chapter deals with estimation, checking and rounding to sensible levels of accuracy and the principles established there are reinforced elsewhere in the text.

In the remaining chapters, calculator techniques are developed and practised in a structured way relevant to a first examination course in mathematics, with reminders given of the appropriate mathematical theory.

Key sequences have been included, taking into account the variety of models of scientific calculator currently on the market. In some situations the given key sequences form part of an investigation into the way particular models operate. Pupils would be well advised to practise consistently on *the same model* of calculator that they will eventually use in their examinations.

The book should prove to be versatile in use. It may be 'dipped into' at almost any stage in the secondary school as topics which involve the use of the calculator are taught. It may also be used as the basis of a more concentrated course for older pupils.

Answers are provided to all of the exercises and in many instances additional information about the solutions is given to benefit in particular those who will study the book without the help of a teacher.

In addition to providing 'Essential Calculator Practice for First Examinations' the book will also lay the foundations of a sound calculator technique for anyone who goes on to study mathematics at a higher level.

I have been greatly assisted by a number of friends and colleagues at Woodhouse School in the writing of this book. I should like to express my gratitude to Mrs R. Walker for her typing of the original script and her patience in dealing with all my amendments, and to Mrs J. Robinson for her artwork ideas. I am also grateful to Mr G. Bennett and Mr L. Morris for their constructive criticism and encouragement at every stage of the project, and to Mr A. Ahmed for his thoroughness in checking the script.

P. Sherran
Tamworth 1986

Note: Where the symbol * appears next to a question or at the start of a section, this indicates a greater level of difficulty appropriate, for example, to the higher levels of GCSE.

CONTENTS

PREFACE   iii

CHAPTER P PRELIMINARY SECTION — APPROXIMATION   1

Decimal places. Foreign currency. Significant figures. Estimation.
Further estimation. Spotting obvious errors. Sensible levels of
accuracy.

CHAPTER 1 BASIC CALCULATIONS   9

Whole number calculations. Money. Correcting errors. Calculating to
the nearest penny. Calculator constants. Foreign currency conversion. Fractions to decimals. Calculating to three significant
figures. Aspects of similarity.

CHAPTER 2 PRIORITY OF OPERATIONS   22

Investigating priority. Changing priority. Priority in practice.
Further questions. Negative number calculations. Simple substitution.
Further questions. The arithmetic mean.

CHAPTER 3 POWERS AND ROOTS   29

Basic calculations. Further calculations. Combined operations.
Pythagoras' theorem. The magnitude of a vector. Direct proportion.
Inverse proportion. Harder examples.

CHAPTER 4 THE CALCULATOR MEMORY   39

Basic operations. A perfect problem? Memory in practice.

CHAPTER 5 PERCENTAGES   44

From fractions to percentages. Percentages of an amount. Increasing
by a percentage. Reducing by a percentage. To express an increase or
decrease as a percentage. Reverse percentages. Converting exam
marks to percentages.

CHAPTER 6 STANDARD FORM   53

What is standard form? Entering standard form on the calculator.
Reading standard form from the display. Further calculations involving standard form. That's torn it!

CHAPTER 7 TRIGONOMETRY   56

Finding sines, cosines and tangents. Finding acute angles. Working
with obtuse angles. Calculation of sides in a right-angled triangle.

CHAPTER 8 USE OF FORMULAE   63

The circle. The sphere. The cylinder. The cone. More areas and
volumes. The gradient of a line. Simple interest. Compound interest.
The sine rule. The cosine rule. The quadratic formula. Iterative
formulae. To conclude with a true story.

ANSWERS   82

Preliminary section –
APPROXIMATION

Imagine that you decide to withdraw from your bank account the interest gained on your savings.

Sometimes we need to round our answers to a *SENSIBLE DEGREE OF ACCURACY.*

P1 Decimal places

The number 3.125 7 includes four figures to the right of the decimal point, i.e. four *decimal places.*

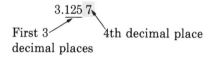

First 3
decimal places

4th decimal place

In order to round the number to three decimal places we consider the figure in the fourth decimal place:

Is it equal to 5 or more?

In this case the answer is *yes* and so we round the figure *up* to make 3.126.

To round the number to two decimal places we consider the figure in the third decimal place, and so on.

This gives 3.125 7 as

3.13 to 2 d.p. (rounded *up*)

and 3.1 to 1 d.p. (rounded *down*, i.e. previous figure left unchanged)

Round each of the following to   a) two decimal places
                                     b) one decimal place

1.	0.372	6.	2.465	11.	19.058
2.	0.468	7.	8.596	12.	16.049
3.	0.529	8.	12.749	13.	0.836 74
4.	0.607	9.	116.854	14.	83.995 2
5.	0.303	10.	7.036	15.	147.397 91

P2   Foreign currency

Note: Rounding to the nearest penny is the same as rounding to 2 d.p. when the amount is given in £.

Given the following exchange rates:

1 franc = £0.083 403,   1 dollar = £0.722 02,   10 lire = £0.039 216

find the value to the nearest penny of

1.	1 franc	5.	20 dollars	9.	30 francs
2.	10 francs	6.	1000 dollars	10.	2000 lire
3.	100 francs	7.	100 lire		
4.	1 dollar	8.	10 000 lire		

P3   Significant figures

The distance of the earth from the sun is often taken to be 93 000 000 miles. This is not the exact distance (which varies throughout the year) and only the first two figures are *significant*. In this case the zeros serve only to give the correct *place value* to the 9 and the 3.

EXAMPLE: The value of 45.037 is shown below rounded to

    a) 4 s.f. **b)** 3 s.f. **c)** 2 s.f. **d)** 1 s.f.

    a) 45.04 (rounded up in much the same way as in section P1)

    b) 45.0 (note in this case the zero *is* signigicant)

    c) 45

    d) 50 (in this case the zero is not a significant figure, but is needed to give the correct place value to the 5)

Round each of the following numbers to

a) three significant figures   **b)** one significant figure

1.	5476	**6.**	17.43	**11.**	0.008 094
2.	81 690	**7.**	6795	**12.**	0.080 07
3.	17 482	**8.**	12.499	**13.**	0.040 03
4.	25 894	**9.**	0.784 62	**14.**	40.03
5.	6741.8	**10.**	0.057 31	**15.**	700 900

P4 Estimation

By rounding the numbers in the questions to one significant figure, find *rough* answers to each of the following:

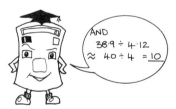

1.	26.6 × 18.7	**8.**	0.671 × 0.793	**15.**	238.6 ÷ 37.2
2.	37.9 × 43.2	**9.**	0.109 × 0.0395	**16.**	8.23 ÷ 18.73
3.	16.81 × 27.42	**10.**	0.0876 × 0.0403	**17.**	3.27 ÷ 49.8
4.	312.7 × 0.937	**11.**	76.8 ÷ 3.71	**18.**	8.69 ÷ 47.6
5.	726.8 × 0.0843	**12.**	8432 ÷ 217	**19.**	391 ÷ 0.187
6.	4629 × 0.026	**13.**	12.75 ÷ 1.94	**20.**	7.23 ÷ 0.006 59
7.	8.462 × 0.003 14	**14.**	18.89 ÷ 3.1		

P5 Further estimation

For addition and subtraction the technique for estimating has to be different. Consider the calculation:

$$8496 + 467 + 84$$

Proceeding as before this would be approximated to:

$$8000 + 500 + 80$$

Technique:

1. Round the largest number to two significant figures.

2. Round the remaining numbers to the *same place value* and then proceed with the calculation.

In this way:	$8496 + 467 + 84$
Becomes:	$8500 + 500 + 100 = 9100$

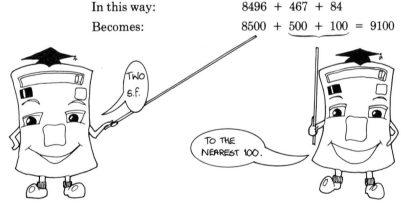

Now estimate:

1. $5632 + 729 + 685$
2. $4867 + 341 + 77$
3. $31.75 + 9.856 + 0.946$
4. $56.218 + 11.73 + 0.0872$
5. $86.49 + 13.72 + 6.035$
6. $4.72 + 1.146 + 0.873$
7. $17.48 + 1.076 + 0.049 + 0.7835$
8. $121.83 + 17.49 + 38.07$

9. $241.92 + 118.59 + 76.43$
10. $12.72 + 141.57 + 16.83$
11. $30.72 + 417.59 + 97.53$
12. $68.54 + 9.83 - 14.72$
13. $176.8 + 38.94 - 87.58$
14. $76\,542 + 6478 - 11\,927$
15. $480\,624 + 57\,276 - 483.972$

P6 Spotting obvious errors

A most important step in any calculation involves checking that the answer is approximately correct. In this way 'obvious' errors can be avoided.

In the following exercise the answers given are either correct or 'obviously' wrong.

Find the *incorrect* statements.

1. $87 \times 39 = 3393$
2. $27 \times 51 = 1877$
3. $412 \times 680 = 28\,016$
4. $3.127 \times 7.849 = 20.543\,823$
5. $0.497 \times 8.472 = 42.105\,84$
6. $0.098 \times 176 = 17.248$
7. $826 \div 35 = 23.6$
8. $512 \div 24.9 = 31.68$
9. $18.13 \div 0.49 = 37$
10. $7.35 \div 0.098 = 75$
11. $16.57 \div 27.83 = 1.679$
12. $8765 + 4176 + 387 = 13\,328$
13. $59.4 + 8.374 - 17.4 = 32.826$
14. $0.725 + 1.943 - 0.318 = 2.35$
15. £47.58 + £8.31 − 36p = £19.89
16. £1.72 + £2.35 + 64p − 37p = £4.34
17. $0.79 \text{ m} + 1.42 \text{ m} + 8.63 \text{ m} = 10.84 \text{ m}$
18. $12.75 \text{ m} + 2.63 \text{ m} + 94 \text{ cm} + 1.86 \text{ m} = 26.64 \text{ m}$
19. $\sqrt{9.47} = 2.8703$
20. $\sqrt{151.29} = 12.3$
21. $(4.7)^2 = 29.02$
22. $(0.32)^2 = 0.1024$
23. $(0.91)^3 = 7.535\,71$
24. $\sqrt{(2.9)^2 + (3.8)^2} = 47.8$
25. $\sqrt{(5.1)^2 + (12.2)^2} = 13.2$
26. $3 \times \sin 67° = 2.762$
27. $15 \times \cos 76° = 36.29$
28. $71.9 \times \tan 45° = 71.9$
29. $2 \times \tan 89° = 114.6$
30. $\dfrac{10}{\sin 32°} = 1.887$

P7 Sensible levels of accuracy

Having finally satisfied ourselves that we have actually arrived at the right answer we are then often faced with the problem of rounding it to an appropriate level of accuracy. In this respect it is advisable to consider calculations based on measurements obtained from practical work *separately* from calculations based on information given in examination questions.

In a practical situation the first thing to consider is the accuracy of the information used in the calculation. For example it would be ridiculous to calculate the length of a side of a triangle to the nearest mm using information accurate only to the nearest m.

If the final answer is to be used in some way then again this may indicate a suitable level of accuracy.

Some practical problems are shown below together with answers given (without working) to the full accuracy of a calculator. Round each answer to the level of accuracy that you consider to be most appropriate in the light of the comments made above.

THIS IS ALL BEYOND ME.

1. In a survey designed to establish the average number of children per family in Staffordshire there were found to be 12 216 children in the sample of 5000 families. Find the average.

   Average number of children per family = 2.443 2

2. In an examination a candidate scores 58 marks out of a possible 74. Calculate his percentage.

   Percentage scored = 78.378 378%

3. A marathon runner measures the length of his stride as 46 inches. Use this measurement as a basis for estimating the number of strides he would take to cover a full marathon course of 26 miles 385 yards.

   Number of strides = 36 113.478

START

1 2 3 4..

25 MILES LATER...

OH NO! I'VE LOST COUNT

BETTER START AGAIN 1 2 3 4...

4. In a class survey 29 pupils were asked about their family pets. In reply 7 pupils said that they did not have any pets. What angle should be used to represent these pupils on a pie chart?

Angle = 86.896 552°

5. A car handbook gives the diameter of a piston as 80.93 mm. Find the equivalent measurement in inches given that 1 mm = 0.039 37 inches.

Equivalent measurement = 3.186 214 1 inches

In an examination we don't normally have the background information necessary to judge for ourselves what level of accuracy is most appropriate and so the required accuracy is often specified in the question. If this is not the case then check the general instructions given on the front cover of the examination paper.

In the absence of any specific instructions the following guidelines are suggested.

a) When dealing with money round your answer to the smallest unit of currency, e.g. the nearest penny.

b) When calculating the angles of a triangle using trigonometry, round to the nearest 0.1°.

c) In other situations, a rule of thumb is to round to three significant figures.

An examiner will not be impressed to find that in your final answer to a problem you have merely copied all of the figures from your calculator display without a second thought.

Some sample examination problems are shown below and once again answers are given to the full accuracy of a calculator. Use the guidelines above to round each answer to an appropriate level of accuracy.

6. Calculate x.

x = 6.850 547 4 cm

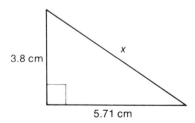

7. A car travels 257 km in $3\frac{1}{2}$ hours. Calculate its average speed.

Average speed = 74.428 571 km/h

8. Find θ.

$\theta = 36.121\ 973°$

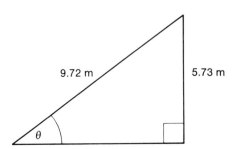

9.2 m and 5.73 m

9. Find the compound interest on £475 invested for three years at 9.3% per annum.

Compound interest = £145.231 91

10. A motorist sets off on a journey of 183 miles with a full tank of petrol. At the end of the journey 4.7 gallons of petrol are required to fill the tank to the same level. Calculate the average rate at which petrol was consumed.

Rate of consumption = 38.936 m.p.g.

1 BASIC CALCULATIONS

1A Whole number calculations

1. $5327 + 16\,725$
2. $8543 - 7249$
3. $2030 - 176$
4. $8312 + 94\,837$
5. $60\,023 - 4738$
6. 24×9
7. 83×52
8. 412×261
9. $1764 \div 4$
10. $23\,643 \div 9$
11. $6631 \div 19$
12. $39\,302 \div 86$
13. $6431 + 789 + 416$
14. $2573 + 17\,241 + 8932$
15. $479 + 826 - 639$
16. $9725 - 496 + 368$
17. $8972 - 531 - 426$
18. $16 \times 24 \times 32$
19. $151 \times 63 \times 27$
20. $1431 \times 62 \div 27$

1B Money

EXAMPLE:

$£23.75 \div 6.25$

In response to the key sequence

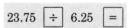

The calculator will display $\boxed{3.8}$ *Only one decimal place*

This must be *written* as £3.80

1. $£7.52 + £25 + £0.83$
2. $£372 + £48.50 - £9.73$
3. $£4.63 - £2.01 + 58\text{p}$
4. $63\text{p} + 97\text{p} + 82\text{p} - £1.48$
5. $£6.32 + 96\text{p} - £2.47$
6. $£52 - £27.33 - 78\text{p}$
7. $46\text{p} + 92\text{p} - £0.38 + £1.52$
8. $£6.72 \times 9$
9. $£12.35 \div 5$
10. $£1.60 \times 10$
11. $£37 \div 10$
12. $42\text{p} \times 100$
13. $£86 \div 100$
14. $£7 \div 100$
15. $£56.32 \div 16$
16. $£42 \times 1.5$
17. $£86 \times 3.2$
18. $£405.84 \div 7.12$
19. $£258.33 \div 6.54$
20. $£6.72 \div 0.8$

1C Correcting errors

Your calculator will have a cancel key which should allow you to make corrections as you go along without the need to start again.

Imagine that in trying to add 3 and 2 together you enter the second number as 4. The following key sequence shows how the mistake can be corrected:

Key: 3 [+] 4 [C] 2 [=]   *Might be labelled CE*

Oops!

Find the key on your calculator which allows the calculation to be made so that the answer 5 is obtained.

Note: This key is only effective when pressed *before* any subsequent

operations [+], [−], [×], [+] or [=]

When two different operation keys are pressed the calculator will ignore the first one.

It is also possible to clear *all previous calculations* either by pressing a different special key or by pressing the cancel key twice, depending on the model of calculator.

In this situation the result obtained above is 2 *not* 5.

Find how to clear all previous calculations on your machine.

Another common error is to enter the wrong operation.

In the last example if the [×] key was pressed instead of the [+] key then this could be corrected as follows:

Key: 3 [×] [+] 2 [=]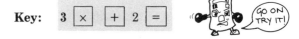

GO ON TRY IT!

A great deal of time and effort can be saved by making use of these error-correcting procedures, as you may appreciate in the next exercise.

1. For each of the calculations given in this question a partly completed key sequence is supplied containing an error at the last step.

   In each case enter the key sequence exactly as given, correct the error and complete the calculation *without* resorting to clearing your machine properly.

   State (i) the steps used to complete the calculation
         (ii) the correct value of the expression.

   a) $16 + 42 + 57 + 83$ Sequence $16 + 42 + 57 + 38$ ...

   b) $471 + 386 + 219 + 127$ Sequence $471 + 386 \times$ ...

   c) $51.2 + 12.7 - 36.9 + 18.5$ Sequence $51.2 + 12.7 - 39.6 +$ ...

   d) $8 \times 3 \times 2 \times 4 \times 5$ Sequence $8 \times 3 \times 2 \times 7$ ...

   e) $4 \times 6 \times 5 \times 3 \times 9$ Sequence $4 \times 6 \times 5 \times 8 \times$ ...

   f) $8.2 + 5.73 + 0.98 + 10.6$ Sequence $8.2 + 5.73 + 9.8 +$ ...

DON'T BLAME ME I JUST FOLLOW YOUR INSTRUCTIONS

2. **CROSS-CHECK:** Use the sub-totals A to D and E to H as a cross-check for finding the grand total.

38.1	62	0.45	5.7	TOTAL A	_____
12.6	3.72	5.91	0.62	TOTAL B	_____
283	14.9	16.72	27.53	TOTAL C	_____
8.01	0.72	12.95	81.52	TOTAL D	_____
Total E	Total F	Total G	Total H		
_____	_____	_____	_____		

3. Details of the transactions of a bank account for the month of June are given below. Calculate the balance at the positions A to G.

Date	Particulars	Credits	Debits	Balance
1.6.85	Balance brought forward			40.23
	Bank Giro credit	600.47		
	526730		18.94	
	Building Society s/o		147.80	(A)
2.6.85	526731		40.00	
	A. Ins. Company s/o		27.53	(B)
9.6.85	526733		96.54	
	Sundry credit	12.00		(C)
10.6.85	526732		38.50	
	526734		6.45	
	Counter cheque		30.00	(D)
15.6.85	526737		40.00	(E)
16.6.85	Transfer from Dep. Acc.	200.00		
	526738		385.50	(F)
25.6.85	526735		12.87	(G)

Find the total credits (H) and the total debits (I) for the month and use these values together with the 'Balance brought forward' to check the final balance (G).

4. Find the totals of these supermarket bills:

a) £	b) £	c) £
3.67	6.49	0.49
1.25	1.38	0.49
0.41	0.27	0.49
0.41	0.39	1.27
0.41	0.72	0.37
0.27	1.61	0.31
2.43	2.59	1.62
1.36	3.42	0.35
1.57	8.16	0.35
0.99	4.27	1.28
0.29	3.12	0.41
5.67	5.59	0.41
1.28	0.41	1.22
0.76	0.39	0.39
3.52	2.76	0.28
2.49	1.47	0.57
0.38	4.28	1.26
0.12	0.39	1.26
1.29	2.26	0.59
5.37	———	0.26
———		0.33
		0.21
		3.52
		1.26
		———

1D Calculating to the nearest penny

1. £7.83 ÷ 5
2. £27.91 ÷ 7
3. £143 ÷ 6
4. £25.63 ÷ 4.7
5. £327 ÷ 8.62
6. £2.56 × 7.3
7. £0.43 × 57.2
8. £16.53 × 1.42
9. £417.63 × 0.72
10. £2352.67 × 1.15
11. 38.7p × 25
12. 5.09p × 637
13. Find the cost of 2.84 m of material at £1.87 per metre.
14. Find the value of 13.7 ounces of sweets at 12p an ounce.
15. How much should be charged for 45.7 litres of petrol at 43p per litre?
16. Calculate the bill for using 857 units of electricity at 6.108p per unit.

The remaining questions in this section require *two* steps to be carried out.

Take care not to do any rounding until the calculation is complete.

ROUNDING TOO EARLY INTRODUCES UNNECESSARY ERROR INTO THE CALCULATION.

17. The cost of a packet of washing powder of net weight 900 g is £1.06. If no reduction is made for larger quantities, calculate the cost of a packet of the same powder of net weight 1.5 kg.

18. Given that the cost of 1.48 m of material is £7.55, find the cost of 2.3 m of the same material.

19. A particular brand of emulsion paint is sold in both 2 litre and 3.5 litre tins. Given that the price of a 3.5 litre tin is £6.31, calculate the cost of a 2 litre tin.

20. A customer wants to buy two videotapes that are normally sold in packs of three for £11.99. If the shopkeeper splits the pack without making any extra charge, how much does the customer pay?

1E Calculator constants

Experiment with your calculator.

Try the following key sequence:

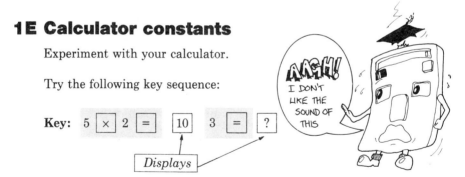

Key: 5 × 2 = 10 3 = ?

Displays

AASH! I DON'T LIKE THE SOUND OF THIS

If the displayed value ? is 15 then your calculator has 'remembered' the instruction to multiply by 5 and will continue to multiply any other numbers that you enter by 5 until you tell it differently.

If the displayed value ? is 3 then try the sequence:

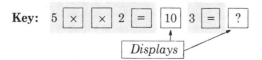

Key: 5 × × 2 = 10 3 = ?

Displays

If again the answer is 3 then you probably have a calculator with a key labelled K. If so, try the sequence

Key: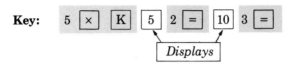

(If that doesn't work, then consult your calculator manual!)

You should now find that if you want to multiply any number by 5 then all you need to do is to enter the number followed by $=$. The process may be repeated for as long as you wish.

The point is most clearly seen by considering an example:

The 31 members of form 5Z carried out a class survey to establish the least popular day of the school week. The results were:

Monday – 14	Thursday – 5
Tuesday – 7	Friday – 2
Wednesday – 3	

It was then decided to illustrate these results using a pie chart. Calculate the angle of each of the sectors to an appropriate level of accuracy.

Angle to represent each pupil $= 360° \div 31 = 11.612\,903°$ (CALC)

The appropriate sector angles may now be found by multiplying each of 14, 7, 3, 5 and 2 by this figure.

1. Complete the solution above by using the constant multiplier facility of your calculator and rounding the results to the nearest degree. (Check that the sum of your final answers $= 360°$.)

2. Carry out a similar survey for your own form and draw the corresponding pie chart.

3. Calculate the angles of a pie chart used to illustrate the following results of a survey in which the members of a class were asked to assess their calculator skills.

Weak – 12	Competent – 5
Fair – 10	Very good – 2

4. A model car is made on a scale of 1:25. Some measurements taken from the model are:

   length 17.2 cm, width 9.2 cm, height 5.48 cm, wheel diameter 2.34 cm.

   Calculate the corresponding measurements of the actual car.

5. A sum of money is to be left in a bank account to gain compound interest over a period of 10 years. At the end of that time the original sum will have grown by a factor of 2.535 39. Calculate to the nearest penny the final amount if the sum originally invested is:

   a) £100 c) £850 e) £16 385
   b) £230 d) £1245

There are many more applications of the constant multiplier. Look out for them in the sections that follow.

Division by a constant is also possible in much the same way, as is the addition and subtraction of a constant. Experiment to find out how they work on *your* calculator.

Now try these.

6. Which of the following numbers are multiples of 147?

   a) 58 149 e) 80 417
   b) 67 325 f) 60 143
   c) 8232 g) 96 726
   d) 54 096

7. Using the information given in question 5, calculate the initial sums invested in order to yield the following amounts after 10 years. Answers to be given to the nearest pound.

   a) £96 d) £2500
   b) £3415 e) £15 700
   c) £1864

8. A Christmas bonus of £85.31 is to be paid to all workers at a toy factory. Calculate the total paid on the following basic earnings:

   a) £97.82 e) £168.56
   b) £112.94 f) £216.39
   c) £131.56 g) £254.76
   d) £122.95

9. A group of holidaymakers find that they have to pay a surcharge of £21.63 for their holiday. Calculate the amount of spending money remaining out of the following amounts:

   a) £187.53 d) £286.92
   b) £207.90 e) £407.80
   c) £141.30

1F Foreign currency conversion

The following exchange rates apply to questions 1 and 2.

1 franc = £0.085 712   1 dollar = £0.731 56   10 lire = £0.038 978

1. Find the value to the nearest penny of:

    a) 27 francs   e) 2386 dollars
    b) 543 francs   f) 5100 lire
    c) 3490 francs   g) 29 800 lire
    d) 765 dollars

2. An American tourist arrives in Britain having already visited France and Italy. He converts 1680 lire, 227 francs and a further 400 dollars into sterling. While in Britain he spends £275 and converts the remainder into dollars before travelling home. Calculate how much he receives to the nearest dollar.

1G Fractions to decimals

EXAMPLE 1: Write $\frac{5}{17}$ as a decimal to 3 decimal places.

Key: 5 $\div$ 17 $=$

Giving   0.294 117 6 = 0.294 (to 3 decimal places)

EXAMPLE 2: Write $6\frac{5}{9}$ as a decimal correct to 3 decimal places.

Key: 6 $+$ 5 $\div$ 9 $=$

Giving 6.555 555 = 6.556 (to 3 decimal places)

OR 6·555 555 6 IF YOUR CALCULATOR ROUNDS THE LAST FIGURE!

If you don't understand why this method of converting mixed numbers into decimals works then take a second look at it after you have worked through Exercise 2A.

Write as decimals correct to 3 d.p.

1. $\dfrac{5}{8}$ 　　6. $\dfrac{5}{6}$ 　　11. $5\dfrac{3}{7}$

2. $\dfrac{7}{11}$ 　　7. $\dfrac{2}{3}$ 　　12. $16\dfrac{2}{9}$

3. $\dfrac{5}{9}$ 　　8. $\dfrac{5}{12}$ 　　13. $12\dfrac{5}{6}$

4. $\dfrac{1}{3}$ 　　9. $\dfrac{9}{16}$ 　　14. $\dfrac{27}{11}$

5. $\dfrac{2}{7}$ 　　10. $\dfrac{17}{23}$ 　　15. $\dfrac{23}{19}$

1H Calculating to three significant figures

EXAMPLES: a) 8.671×4.153

$= 36.01\ldots$ (CALC)

$= 36.0$ (3 s.f.)

Est $9 \times 4 = 36$

a) $\dfrac{9}{17}$ of 8.35

$= 4.420\ldots$ (CALC)

$= 4.42$ (3 s.f.)

Est $\frac{1}{2}$ of $8.4 = 4.2$

Key: 9 ÷ 17 × 8.35 =

Note: In the examples shown above only the information required to round the final answer to 3 s.f. has been copied from the display, followed by ... to indicate that some figures have been omitted.

This approach will be used throughout the rest of the book and it is recommended that you adopt this style when showing your own working.

1. 2.37×1.49
2. 86.3×2.72
3. 2.69×0.735
4. 0.372×0.0148
5. 5600×861
6. 239×547
7. 5.71×2.85
8. $8.67 \div 19.9$
9. $4.32 \div 0.57$
10. $0.073 \div 0.0019$

11. $\dfrac{5}{9}$ of 12.2
12. $\dfrac{8}{15}$ of 0.67
13. $\dfrac{2}{7}$ of 5.68
14. $\dfrac{11}{12}$ of 77.3
15. $\dfrac{9}{16}$ of 157

1I Aspects of similarity

EXAMPLE: Triangle X has sides of length 5 cm, 3 cm and 7 cm. Triangle Y has sides of length 8.1 cm, 13.5 cm and 19.9 cm. Are they similar?

Calculation of the appropriate ratios yields:

$$\frac{8.1}{3} = 2.7, \quad \frac{13.5}{5} = 2.7, \quad \frac{19.9}{7}$$
$$= 2.8\ldots$$

Since the three ratios are not equal it follows that X and Y are *not* similar.

Note: If the longest side of triangle Y was changed to 18.9 cm, then the ratios would all be equal and the triangles would be similar.

The common ratio of 2.7 could then be regarded as the scale factor of the enlargement that would map triangle X on to triangle Y.

1. Which of the triangles shown below is similar to triangle A?

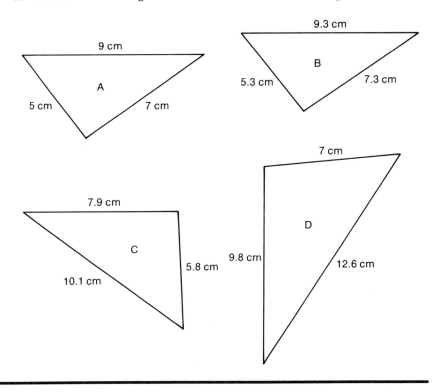

2. In the diagram below, the shaded triangle may be mapped on to each of the other triangles by an enlargement. In each case give the value of the scale factor and find the unknown measurements.

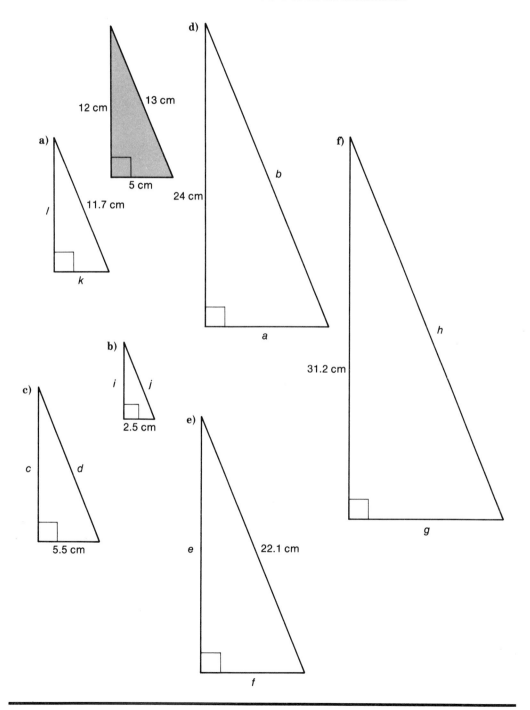

3. Towns A, B, C, D are linked by road as shown in the diagram. The measurements given are taken from a map drawn to a scale of 1 cm to 3.5 km.

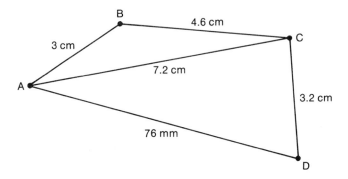

a) Calculate the corresponding distances between the towns.

b) A motorist travelling from town D to town B by the shortest route is forced to make a diversion at town C which takes him through town A. How much further does he have to travel because of the diversion?

c) Express the scale of the map in the form 1:n.

4. The measurements on the diagram below are given correct to the nearest $\frac{1}{32}$ inch.

a) Convert all of the measurements to centimetres and millimetres.

b) Given that the diagram represents a field on a scale of 1:1000, give the corresponding measurements of the field to the nearest metre.

(Take 1 inch = 2.54 cm)

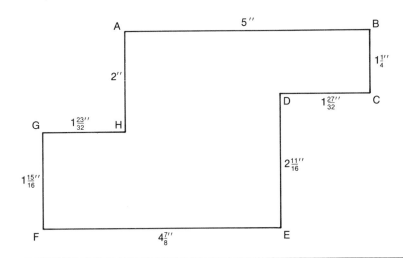

5. A map is drawn to a scale of 1:50 000

   a) Find the actual distance between two towns drawn 17 cm apart on the map.

   b) The shortest distance by road between the same towns is 11.5 km. What would be the corresponding distance on the map?

   c) The map also shows a reservoir which covers an area of 4.8 km^2. Calculate the corresponding area on the map.

6. From a point at ground level, the top of a tree and the top of a fence post of height 1.3 m are observed to be in line. The horizontal distance from the point of observation to the post and to the tree are 1.8 m and 15.7 m respectively.

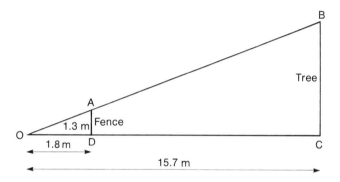

   a) Calculate the height of the tree by comparing $\dfrac{OC}{OD}$ and $\dfrac{BC}{AD}$.

   b) Check your answer to part (**a**) by comparing $\dfrac{AD}{OD}$ and $\dfrac{BC}{OC}$.

2 PRIORITY OF OPERATIONS

2A Investigating priority

Consider the following calculation:

$$3 + 4 + 2$$

The key sequence and corresponding display are shown in the table below:

KEY	3	+	4	+	2	=
DISPLAY	3	3	4	7	2	9

Previous addition carried out at this stage.

For each of the following questions

(i)   Find the value *without* using the calculator.

(ii) Draw the corresponding key/display table.

(iii) Compare your answer with the calculator answer.

(iv) You will find it easier to make the comparison if you position the tables in a vertical line.

1. a) $8 + 2 + 3$
    b) $8 + 2 \times 3$
    c) $8 + 2 - 3$
    d) $8 - 3 + 2$
    e) $8 - 2 \times 3$

2. a) $24 - 6 - 2$
    b) $24 - 6 \div 2$
    c) $24 + 6 \div 2$
    d) $24 \div 6 \times 2$
    e) $24 \times 2 \div 6$

2B Changing priority

Compare the key/display table shown below for the calculation
$24 - (6 - 2)$ with your solution to question 2(a) of Section 2A.

KEY	24	−	(	6	−	2	)	=
DISPLAY	24	24		6	6	2	4	20

The display at this stage depends on the model of calculator but does not affect the calculation.

The subtraction inside the brackets is carried out first.

Construct the key/display tables for the following calculations and describe the effect of the brackets in each case.

1. $16 - (8 - 2)$ 4. $35 \div (4 + 3)$

2. $5 \times (7 - 3)$ 5. $14 - 3 \times (7 - 5)$

3. $12 \div (9 - 5)$ 6. $35 \div (12 - (9 - 4))$

Don't forget to close BOTH pairs of brackets before you press $\boxed{=}$

Note: In some situations it is easier to bring about a change in priority by using the $\boxed{=}$ key.

Consider the following calculation:

$$\frac{8 + 4}{2}$$

Since the addition must be carried out first it would be *incorrect* to key:

Key: 8 $\boxed{+}$ 4 $\boxed{\div}$ 2 $\boxed{=}$

as the calculator would carry out the *division* first.

One method is to key

Key: $\boxed{(}$ 8 $\boxed{+}$ 4 $\boxed{)}$ $\boxed{\div}$ 2 $\boxed{=}$

but the shortest key sequence is

Key: 8 $\boxed{+}$ 4 $\boxed{=}$ $\boxed{\div}$ 2 $\boxed{=}$

2C Priority in practice

In this exercise you will need to use the results obtained in the last two sections. Some questions will require the introduction of brackets.

1. $\dfrac{26 + 9}{7}$

2. $21.5 + 38 \div 4$

3. $\dfrac{57}{11 + 8}$

4. $\dfrac{45}{3 \times 6} + 1.5$

5. $\dfrac{121 - 36}{17}$

6. $\dfrac{90}{5 \times 8} - \dfrac{5}{4}$

7. $\dfrac{53 + 35}{31 - 9}$

8. $\dfrac{87}{11 + 6 \times 3}$

9. $8.25 - \left(17 - \dfrac{47}{4}\right)$

10. $16 \times \left(\dfrac{7}{4} + \dfrac{5}{8}\right)$

11. $(3.7 + 4.8) \times (2.3 + 5.7)$

12. $\dfrac{15 \times 24}{27 + 18}$

13. $\dfrac{121.8 - 22.4}{10 - 2.9}$

14. $25.7 - (29.3 - 14.6)$

15. $\dfrac{81.2 - (42.7 + 23.5)}{17.1 - (12.9 + 1.2)}$

16. Find the value of 14 times the sum of 18.7 and 29.8

17. Divide the positive difference between 24.1 and 81.7 by 3.2

18. Add 16.19 to the product of 2.3 and 4.7

19. Divide 829.5 by the sum of 15.62 and 8.08

20. Multiply the sum of 16.59 and 13.41 by 5.9

21. Divide the sum of 197.6 and 248.8 by the product of 2.4 and 7.75

22. Subtract the positive difference between 58.72 and 31.06 from the sum of 46.59 and 28.07

23. Multiply the sum of 0.79 and 0.61 by the sum of 3.67 and 11.33

24. Divide the product of 15.7 and 3.8 by the sum of 0.567 and 2.573

25. Subtract the sum of 38.579 and 14.515 from the product of 18.7 and 5.62

2D Further questions

Calculate the value of the following correct to 3 s.f. using brackets where necessary. In each case check your answer by estimation.

1. $\dfrac{5.61 + 18.7}{6.9}$

Est $\dfrac{6 + 19}{7}$

$= \dfrac{25}{7} = 3.\,(\text{something})$

2. $\dfrac{5.73}{2.79 + 1.8}$

3. $5 + \dfrac{2.9}{1.73}$

4. $\dfrac{8.6}{12.9} + \dfrac{17.2}{3.95}$

EVEN A VERY ROUGH ESTIMATE IS BETTER THAN HAVING NO IDEA ABOUT THE SIZE OF THE ANSWER.

5. $\dfrac{147}{8 \times 17 + 9}$

6. $\dfrac{8.74 - 2.67}{25.8 - 23.7}$

7. $\dfrac{5.86 \times 12.3 + 7.2}{7.64 \times 2.38}$

9. $\dfrac{26.5}{5.7} \div \dfrac{8.63}{4.37}$

8. $\dfrac{8.72}{4.6} \times \dfrac{12.7}{3.82}$

10. $\dfrac{16.7 - (9.81 - 4.7)}{2.54 + 1.6}$

2E Negative number calculations

EXAMPLES: a) $-6 - 5$ b) $4 - -3$

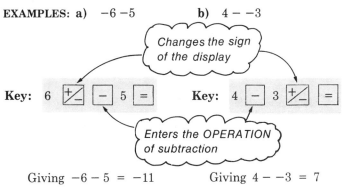

Changes the sign of the display

Key: 6 $\boxed{+/-}$ $\boxed{-}$ 5 $\boxed{=}$ **Key:** 4 $\boxed{-}$ 3 $\boxed{+/-}$ $\boxed{=}$

Enters the OPERATION of subtraction

Giving $-6 - 5 = -11$ Giving $4 - -3 = 7$

> *Note the difference between entering the operation of subtraction and the negative sign of a number.*

First work these out mentally and then use the calculator

1. $6 - 9$	4. $-7 + 3$	7. $3 + -1$
2. $-2 + 5$	5. $-8 + 8$	8. $5 - -4$
3. $-4 - 6$	6. $-100 + 1$	9. $6 + -9$

10.	$-3 + -4$	**22.**	$-25 \div 5$
11.	$-6 + -2$	**23.**	$-32 \div 16$
12.	$-8 - -5$	**24.**	$-3 \times (-2 + 4)$
13.	$-5 - -7$	**25.**	$7 \times (-3 - 2)$
14.	$3 - (-5 + 1)$	**26.**	$3 + 5 \times (-6 + 4)$
15.	$-4 - (-3 + 8)$	**27.**	$-5 - 4 \times (-6 + -2)$
16.	4×-5	**28.**	$-16 + 12 - 14 + 2 \times -3$
17.	-3×6	**29.**	$\dfrac{-3 + 19}{-8}$
18.	-4×-2		
19.	5×-3	**30.**	$\dfrac{-3 - 5}{7 - 11}$
20.	$-3 \times -2 \times -4$		
21.	$16 \div -8$		

2F Simple substitution

Substitute $a = 3$, $b = -5$, $c = -2$ in the following:

1.	$\dfrac{a + b}{c}$	**6.**	$a - c$
		7.	$a - b - c$
2.	ab		
3.	abc	**8.**	$\dfrac{a + b}{c} - b$
4.	$\dfrac{a - b}{c}$	**9.**	$\dfrac{bc - ac}{b + a}$
5.	$a + b + c$	**10.**	$(a - b)\,(a + c)$

2G Further questions

Given that $p = -7.39$, $q = 4.71$, $r = -6.85$, evaluate the following expressions correct to 3 s.f.

1.	pq	**6.**	$\dfrac{3p + 2q}{p + q}$
2.	$pr - q$		
		7.	$\dfrac{p}{q} - \dfrac{r}{q - 3}$
3.	$\dfrac{p + q}{r}$		
		8.	$(p + q)\,(r + 7)$
4.	$p(q + r)$	**9.**	$p(q - r) + 7.2\,(p + 6)$
5.	$\dfrac{p}{q - r}$	**10.**	$\dfrac{pqr}{p + q + r}$

2H The arithmetic mean

An average is a representative value, i.e. one figure may be used to represent a whole collection of numbers.

There are several methods of obtaining a representative value but perhaps the most commonly used is the arithmetic mean.

$$\text{Arithmetic Mean Value } = \frac{\text{Sum of all values}}{\text{Number of values considered}}$$

1. Calulate the mean of:
    a) 5, 7, 11, 9, 10, 13, 8, 9
    b) 2.7, 5.3, 6.1, 4.8, 5.7, 3.6
    c) 42, 31, 29, 50, 37, 44, 33
    d) 0.9, 0.74, 0.8, 0.32, 0.49
    e) 121, 143, 116, 139, 127, 109, 137, 158, 136, 124
    f) 47, 16, 0, 12, 10, 18, 32, 69
    g) 3, 8, 0, 10, 5, 2, 0, 6, 9, 11
    h) 5.8, 2.6, −3.7, −1.9, 2.4, −4.2, 6
    i) −8, −7, −9, 5, 1, 3, −12, −5
    j) −8.8, −7.8, −9.8, 4.2, 0.2, 2.2, −12.8, −5.8
    k) −16, −14, −18, 10, 2, 6, −24, −10
    l) −976, −842, −881, −847, −903, −728

2. The mean of 9 numbers is 7.6. When an extra figure is included the new mean is 8 what is the extra figure?

3. The mean of 59 numbers is 4.5. What is the least positive value of a 60th number that will make the new mean a whole number?

4. Five of the workers at a small factory earn £86.42 per week. A further ten people earn £97.81 per week and the two joint owners of the factory each earn £387.25 per week.
    a) Calculate the weekly wage bill for the factory.
    b) Calculate the mean weekly wage.
    c) Do you think that the mean wage is a good representation of the weekly earnings at the factory?

5. A die was thrown 50 times and the results are shown in the table below:

Score	1	2	3	4	5	6
Frequency	8	6	10	11	9	6

    Calculate the mean score.

6. The number of hours overtime worked by the employees of a firm in one week are shown in the table:

Hours overtime	0	4	8	12	16	20
Number of employees	23	5	11	14	8	6

Calculate:

a) The total number of man-hours worked in overtime.

b) The total number of employees.

c) The mean number of extra hours worked by all of the employees.

Given that a basic week consists of 40 working hours what is the mean number of hours worked by all of the employees?

7. In a class survey the heights of the members of form 1X were recorded as shown below. All measurements are in metres.

1.29	1.31	1.48	1.26	1.43
1.42	1.28	1.31	1.46	1.32
1.34	1.28	1.21	1.39	1.40
1.51	1.54	1.37	1.46	1.39
1.37	1.47	1.41	1.38	1.43
1.46	1.39	1.38	1.52	1.37

Calculate the mean height of the pupils in the form.

8. Form 4X also did a height survey but recorded their results in a different way:

Height in metres	1.30 – 1.40	1.40 – 1.50	1.50 – 1.60	1.60 – 1.70	1.70 – 1.80	1.80 – 1.90
Frequency	2	4	9	10	5	3

Anyone whose height fell on one of the interval boundaries was included in the higher interval.

Use the mid value of each interval as a representative value in order to estimate the mean height of the pupils in 4X to the nearest 5 cm.

3 POWERS AND ROOTS

Your calculator will be equipped with a variety of keys to enable you to calculate powers and roots. In order to make some of these keys operate you will have to press a second function (2nd F) or inverse (INV) key first.

Some expressions involving powers and roots are given below together with key sequences that will require some investigation to make them work on your machine.

Where the symbol $\boxed{*}$ appears in a key sequence this indicates that you *may* need to press a (2nd F) or (INV) key.

Experiment until you obtain the right results.

a) 5^2 **Key:** $\boxed{5}$ $\boxed{*}$ $\boxed{x^2}$

b) $\sqrt{81}$ **Key:** $\boxed{81}$ $\boxed{*}$ $\boxed{\sqrt{}}$

> The reciprocal key
> $\frac{1}{x} = x^{-1}$

c) $\frac{1}{4}$ **Key:** $\boxed{4}$ $\boxed{*}$ $\boxed{\frac{1}{x}}$

Note: When the $\boxed{x^2}$, $\boxed{\sqrt{}}$ or $\boxed{\frac{1}{x}}$ keys are used they operate on the displayed value immediately without the need to press $\boxed{=}$

Some calculators are fitted with $\boxed{x^3}$ and $\boxed{\sqrt[3]{}}$ which operate as above but more generally higher powers and roots are calculated as follows:

> Possibly x^y

d) 2^4 **Key:** $\boxed{2}$ $\boxed{Y^x}$ $\boxed{4}$ $\boxed{=}$

e) $\sqrt[3]{64}$ **Key:** $\boxed{64}$ $\boxed{*}$ $\boxed{\sqrt[x]{Y}}$ $\boxed{3}$ $\boxed{=}$

> Possibly $x^{\frac{1}{y}}$ or even y^x again!

3A Basic calculations

Now try these. In each case you should be able to check the answer mentally:

1.	4^2	17.	5^3	32.	$\dfrac{1}{100}$
2.	7^2	18.	3^4		
3.	10^2	19.	2^5	33.	$\dfrac{1}{16}$
4.	6^2	20.	8^3		
5.	8^2	21.	10^6		
6.	12^2	22.	6^3	34.	$\dfrac{1}{\left(\dfrac{1}{16}\right)}$
7.	$\sqrt{64}$	23.	4^5		
8.	$\sqrt{9}$	24.	$\sqrt[3]{8}$	35.	$\dfrac{1}{\left(\dfrac{1}{8}\right)}$
9.	$\sqrt{49}$	25.	$\sqrt[3]{27}$		
10.	$\sqrt{121}$	26.	$\sqrt[3]{1000}$	36.	$(-3)^2$
11.	$\sqrt{169}$	27.	$\sqrt[4]{10\,000}$		
12.	$\sqrt{100}$	28.	$\sqrt[4]{81}$	37.	$\dfrac{1}{-4}$
13.	$\sqrt{10\,000}$	29.	$\sqrt[5]{32}$	38.	$(-2)^4$
14.	$\sqrt{2500}$	30.	$\dfrac{1}{2}$	39.	$(-10)^5$
15.	$\sqrt{490\,000}$			40.	$(-5)^3$
16.	2^3	31.	$\dfrac{1}{8}$		

Many calculators cannot cope with raising a negative number to a power greater than 2, in which case the signs will have to be worked out separately.

YOU MAY HAVE TO SORT THE SIGNS OUT YOURSELF IN QUESTIONS 38-40

3B Further calculations

A good way to check the results of some types of calculation is to reverse the process and so obtain the number first entered.

For example try the key sequence $\boxed{1}\ \boxed{\div}\ \boxed{3}\ \boxed{=}$

Now without clearing the display key $\boxed{\times}\ \boxed{3}\ \boxed{=}$

Some calculators will display 1 as expected and others will display 0.999 . . . . If your calculator displays 0.999 . . . then you must remember to allow for a slight rounding error in some calculations when reversing the process.

Note: When a number is raised to some power the process may be reversed by calculating the corresponding root, and vice versa.

However, when a reciprocal is found using the $\frac{1}{x}$ key, the process is reversed by pressing the $\frac{1}{x}$ key again (see questions 34, 35 of Section 3A).

TO BE PRECISE, THE FUNCTION $x \rightarrow \frac{1}{x}$ IS SELF-INVERSE.

Evaluate the following correct to 3 s.f. and check the answers by reversing the process.

1. 8.735^2

2. $\sqrt{98.47}$

3. 12.83^2

4. $\sqrt{157.9}$

5. 2.73^3

6. 0.71^3

7. $\sqrt{0.094}$

8. $\sqrt[3]{59.6}$

9. $\sqrt[3]{0.0142}$

10. $\sqrt[4]{857.93}$

11. 0.581^2

12. $\frac{1}{0.786}$

13. $\frac{1}{0.0274}$

14. $6.73^{4.1}$

15. $2.39^{3.7}$

3C Combined operations

> Calculation of powers and roots takes priority over the operations of $\boxed{+}$, $\boxed{-}$, $\boxed{\times}$ and $\boxed{\div}$

EXAMPLES:

a) $\sqrt{9 + 16}$ **Key:** $\boxed{9}$ $\boxed{+}$ $\boxed{16}$ $\boxed{=}$ $\boxed{*}$ $\boxed{\sqrt{}}$

Note how the $\boxed{=}$ is used so that the addition is carried out first.

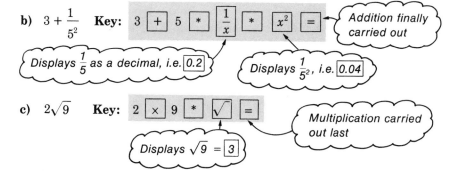

b) $3 + \dfrac{1}{5^2}$ **Key:** $\boxed{3}$ $\boxed{+}$ $\boxed{5}$ $\boxed{*}$ $\boxed{\frac{1}{x}}$ $\boxed{*}$ $\boxed{x^2}$ $\boxed{=}$ ← *Addition finally carried out*

Displays $\frac{1}{5}$ as a decimal, i.e. $\boxed{0.2}$

Displays $\frac{1}{5^2}$, i.e. $\boxed{0.04}$

c) $2\sqrt{9}$ **Key:** $\boxed{2}$ $\boxed{\times}$ $\boxed{9}$ $\boxed{*}$ $\boxed{\sqrt{}}$ $\boxed{=}$ → *Multiplication carried out last*

Displays $\sqrt{9}$ = $\boxed{3}$

*May need (2nd F) or (INV) key.

The answers to questions 1 to 10 may be expressed exactly and should be checked by mental calculation. The remaining answers should be given to 3 s.f. and checked by estimation.

1. $3 + 4^2$
2. $(3 + 4)^2$
3. 3×5^2
4. $4\sqrt{25}$
5. $\sqrt{4 \times 25}$
6. $\sqrt{20 + 16}$
7. $20 + \sqrt{16}$
8. $9 - \dfrac{1}{5}$
9. $\dfrac{1}{9 - 5}$
10. $3 - \dfrac{1}{2^2}$
11. $\sqrt{16.7 + 12.5}$

12. $41.3 + 6.9^2$
13. $\dfrac{1}{2.45^3}$
14. $3\sqrt{3}$
15. $\dfrac{1}{9.2} - \dfrac{1}{12.8}$
16. 3.14×8.6^2
17. $\sqrt{15.7^2 - 8.9^2}$
18. $\dfrac{12.8}{6.7 \times 4.2^2}$
19. $15.3 - \sqrt{16.8}$
20. $\dfrac{1}{\sqrt[4]{81.6 - 23.9}}$

3D Pythagoras' theorem

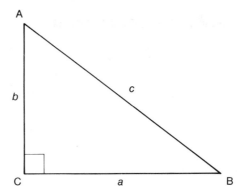

In any right-angled triangle the square on the hypotenuse is equal to the sum of the squares on the other two sides.

In relation to the diagram above the theorem may be expressed algebraically as

$$c^2 = a^2 + b^2$$

It follows that calculation of one of the shorter sides involves *subtracting* the appropriate squares,

i.e. $$b^2 = c^2 - a^2 \qquad \text{and} \qquad a^2 = c^2 - b^2$$

EXAMPLE:

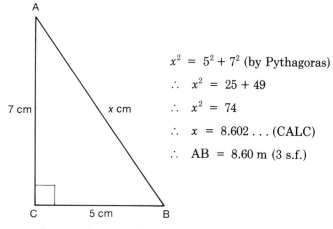

$x^2 = 5^2 + 7^2$ (by Pythagoras)

$\therefore \quad x^2 = 25 + 49$

$\therefore \quad x^2 = 74$

$\therefore \quad x = 8.602\ldots$ (CALC)

$\therefore \quad AB = 8.60$ m (3 s.f.)

Avoid 'silly' answers by carrying out the following checks:

a) Make sure that the hypotenuse (side opposite the right angle) *is* the longest side of the triangle.

b) Add the lengths of the two shorter sides which must then be *greater* than the length of the hypotenuse.

1. Calculate the unknown sides in the triangles below.

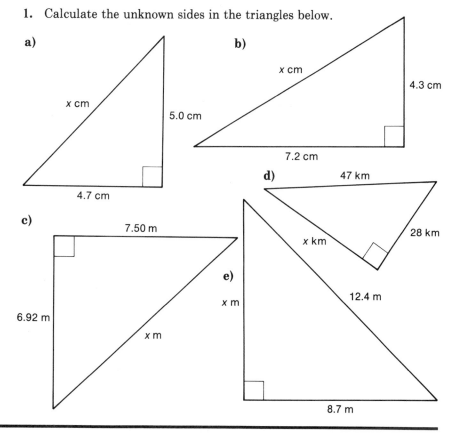

2. Calculate the length of the diagonal of a square of side 8.0 cm.

3. The diagonal of a square measures 4.6 m. Calculate its area.

*4. The internal measurements of a box are 38 cm by 32 cm by 45 cm.

   Is it possible for a thin stick of length 65 cm to fit in the box? Explain your answer.

The converse of Pythagoras' theorem is also true.

If the sides of a triangle are such that the square on one side is equal to the sum of the squares on the other two sides then the angle included by these sides is a right angle.

5. Determine which of the following sets of measurements corresponds to a right-angled triangle:

   a) 6.2 cm, 3.8 cm, 4.6 cm.   **c)** 16 km, 12.3 km, 8.9 km

   b) 2 m, 4.8 m, 5.2 m   **d)** 10.8 cm, 18 cm, 14.4 cm.

3E The magnitude of a vector

In general the magnitude or the length of a vector $\begin{pmatrix} x \\ y \end{pmatrix}$ is given by

$$\sqrt{x^2 + y^2}$$

a result which is clearly based on Pythagoras' theorem.

EXAMPLE: Find the magnitude of the vector $\begin{pmatrix} 5 \\ -3 \end{pmatrix}$

Magnitude $= \sqrt{5^2 + (-3)^2} = \sqrt{34}$

$\qquad\qquad\quad = 5.830 \ldots$ (CALC)

$\qquad\qquad\quad = 5.83$ (to 3 s.f.)

Find the magnitude of these vectors:

1. $\begin{pmatrix} 6 \\ -2 \end{pmatrix}$ 3. $\begin{pmatrix} 5 \\ 8 \end{pmatrix}$ 5. $\begin{pmatrix} -11 \\ 7 \end{pmatrix}$

2. $\begin{pmatrix} -7 \\ 4 \end{pmatrix}$ 4. $\begin{pmatrix} -6 \\ -4 \end{pmatrix}$

Some vectors are shown in the diagram below. Write each vector in the form $\begin{pmatrix} x \\ y \end{pmatrix}$ and find its magnitude.

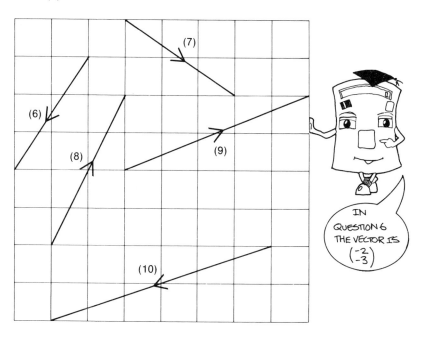

*3F Direct proportion

If the *ratio* of y to x is constant then y is said to vary in direct proportion to x.

The notation $y \propto x$ is used to represent 'y is proportional to x' and we may write

$$\frac{y}{x} = k \quad \text{or} \quad y = kx$$

where k is known as a constant of proportionality. Depending on the situation, k may have its own units.

EXAMPLE 1: A quantity y varies in direct proportion to a quantity x. Given that $y = 9.72$ when $x = 3.6$ find y when $x = 5.3$.

Since the ratio of y to x must be constant

$$\frac{y}{5.3} = \frac{9.72}{3.6} \quad \Rightarrow \quad y = 5.3 \times \frac{9.72}{3.6}$$

$$\Rightarrow \quad y = 14.31 \qquad \text{(CALC)}$$

EXAMPLE 2: Repeat example 1 given that $y \propto x^2$. Give your final answer to 2 d.p.

$$\frac{y}{(5.3)^2} = \frac{9.72}{(3.6)^2} \Rightarrow y = (5.3)^2 \times \frac{9.72}{(3.6)^2}$$

$$\Rightarrow y = 21.067 \qquad \text{(CALC)}$$

$$\Rightarrow y = 21.07 \qquad \text{(2 d.p.)}$$

THESE BRACKETS HAVE BEEN INCLUDED FOR CLARITY BUT ARE NOT ESSENTIAL.

1. In each of the following assume that $y \propto x$ and find the value of y for the value of x given. Answers to be rounded to 3 s.f. where necessary.

   a) $y = 24.36$ when $x = 5.8$
   $(x = 6.7)$

   b) $y = 1.48$ when $x = 18.5$
   $(x = 29.6)$

   c) $y = 87.1$ when $x = 2.6$
   $(x = 15.3)$

   d) $y = 0.731$ when $x = 0.47$
   $(x = 0.38)$

2. Repeat question 1 with $y \propto x^2$

3. Repeat question 1 with $y \propto \sqrt{x}$

4. The surface area of a sphere is directly proportional to the square of its radius.

   A sphere of radius 2.3 cm has a surface area of 66.48 cm^2. Find the surface area of a sphere with radius a) 5.9 cm b) 6.9 cm (Answers to 3 s.f.)

5. The distance it is possible to see on a clear day varies directly as the square root of the height above sea level.

   At a height of 2 m above sea level it is possible to see 6 km.

   a) Without using your calculator find the distance it is possible to see from a height of 8 m.

   b) Using your calculator find the maximum distance for a height of 10 m.

*3G Inverse proportion

If the *product* of y and x is constant then we say that y is inversely proportional to x which is written as $y \propto \dfrac{1}{x}$

It follows that $xy = k$ or $y = \dfrac{k}{x}$

where k is again a constant of proportionality.

EXAMPLE 1: Given that y is inversely proportional to x and that when $x = 4.2$, $y = 3.6$ find y when $x = 6.3$

Since the product remains constant

$6.3 \times y = 4.2 \times 3.6$

$\Rightarrow \quad y = \dfrac{4.2 \times 3.6}{6.3}$

$\Rightarrow \quad y = 2.4$ (CALC)

EXAMPLE 2: Repeat example 1 given that $y \propto \dfrac{1}{x^2}$

$(6.3)^2 \times y = (4.2)^2 \times 3.6$

$\Rightarrow \quad y = \dfrac{(4.2)^2 \times 3.6}{(6.3)^2}$

$\Rightarrow \quad y = 1.6$ (CALC)

1. In each of the following assume that $y \propto \dfrac{1}{x}$ and find the value of y for the given value of x. Round to 3 s.f. where necessary.

    a) $y = 25$ when $x = 4.7$
       $(x = 1.88)$

    b) $y = 38.4$ when $x = 17$
       $(x = 27.2)$

    c) $y = 128.8$ when $x = 0.94$
       $(x = 0.658)$

    d) $y = 0.47$ when $x = 12.2$
       $(x = 9.4)$

2. Repeat question 1 with $y \propto \dfrac{1}{x^2}$

3. Repeat question 1 with $y \propto \dfrac{1}{\sqrt{x}}$

4. For a given volume the length of a cylinder is inversely proportional to the square of the radius.

   A metal cylinder of radius 4.3 cm and length 12.1 cm is melted down and recast to make a cylinder of radius 3.7 cm. Calculate the length of the new cylinder to the nearest mm.

5. For a particle starting from rest and moving with constant acceleration, the time taken to cover a fixed distance is inversely proportional to the square root of the acceleration.

   When the acceleration is 3 m/s², the time taken is 12 s. Find correct to 3 s.f. the time taken to cover the same distance with an acceleration of 2 m/s².

*3H Harder examples

Evaluate to 3 s.f.

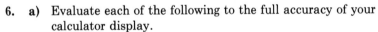

IF YOU LIKE A CHALLENGE TRY THESE.

1. $(3.81)^{-\frac{1}{2}}$
2. $(4.67)^{\frac{2}{3}}$
3. $(0.072)^{-\frac{1}{4}}$
4. $\left((5.2)^{-\frac{1}{3}} + (2.7)^{-\frac{1}{2}}\right)^{-\frac{1}{4}}$
5. $(3.82)^{-\frac{2}{3}} \times (0.012)^{-\frac{1}{5}} \times (3.2)^{\sqrt{3}}$
6. **a)** Evaluate each of the following to the full accuracy of your calculator display.

   (i) $A = \sqrt{0.5}$
   (ii) $B = \sqrt{0.5 + 0.5A}$
   (iii) $C = \sqrt{0.5 + 0.5B}$
   (iv) $D = \sqrt{0.5 + 0.5C}$
   (v) $x = 0.5 \times A \times B \times C \times D$

   b) Using the value of x obtained above calculate $\frac{1}{x}$ to 3 s.f.

   The sequence of instructions given in Question 6 may be extended and the corresponding values of $\frac{1}{x}$ will be found to approximate ever more closely to the value of π. However, the process may be greatly simplified by making use of the calculator memory as shown in Question *11 of Section 4C.

4 THE CALCULATOR MEMORY

4A Basic operations

This section is designed to help you familiarise yourself with the use of the memory keys so that you will have confidence in using them with a calculation. Different models of calculator may have different symbols on the memory keys. Later in the book, those on Casio models have been used.

Carry out the following instructions and at each stage *check that the calculator gives the expected result.*

Instructions	*Notes*
1. Display the number 7 and enter it into the memory.	Depending on the model of calculator use the: $\boxed{\text{Min}}$, $\boxed{x \rightarrow M}$ or $\boxed{\text{STO}}$ key You will *probably* find that the letter 'M' appears in the top left-hand corner of the display to indicate that a number is now stored in the memory.
2. Clear the display.	This does not affect the value stored in the memory.
3. Recall the contents of the memory to the display.	Press the $\boxed{\text{MR}}$, $\boxed{\text{RM}}$ or $\boxed{\text{RCL}}$ key as appropriate. The 7 will re-appear without affecting the value stored in the memory.
4. Add 3 to the contents of the memory.	**Key:** 3 $\boxed{\text{M+}}$ or 3 $\boxed{\text{SUM}}$
5. Recall the contents of the memory to the display.	As for instruction (3). Display should now show 10.

6. Subtract 4 from the contents of the memory.

Key: 4 $\boxed{M-}$, if your calculator has an $\boxed{M-}$ key, if not then you can achieve the same result by *adding* -4 to the memory.

i.e. **Key:** 4 $\boxed{+/-}$ *$\boxed{M+}$

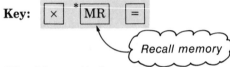

Add to memory as for instruction (4)

7. Recall the contents of the memory to the display.

(Should now display 6).

8. Display 5

Just press the 5 key. There is no need to cancel the display.

9. Multiply display by number contained in memory.

Key: $\boxed{\times}$ *$\boxed{MR}$ $\boxed{=}$

Recall memory

(Should now display 30)

10. Subtract 2× number in memory from display.

Key: $\boxed{-}$ 2 $\boxed{\times}$ *$\boxed{MR}$ $\boxed{=}$

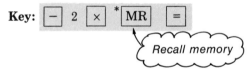

Recall memory

(Should now display 18)

11. Divide display by number in memory.

Key: $\boxed{\div}$ *$\boxed{MR}$ $\boxed{=}$

Recall memory

12. Replace number in memory with that shown on display.

Just use the

$\boxed{Min}$, $\boxed{x \to M}$ or $\boxed{STO}$

key as in instruction (1)

The new number, i.e. 3, will now be stored in the memory and the old number, i.e. 6, will be lost.

*Use key appropriate to your calculator. See p. 39.

13. Clear the display.

14. Recall contents of   Should display 3.
memory to the
display.

15. Clear the memory.   Clear the display first and then use
the

                  $\boxed{\text{Min}}$, $\boxed{x{\rightarrow}M}$ or $\boxed{\text{STO}}$ key

                  again as appropriate.

16. Check that the   The memory indicator 'M' should
memory is clear.   disappear.

                  If your calculator does not have a
                  memory indicator then press the
                  memory recall button and the dis-
                  play should still show zero.

Now work through the instructions again using numbers of your own
choice. If possible try to manage without referring to the notes, but it is
most important to *check that the calculator responds as you expect.*

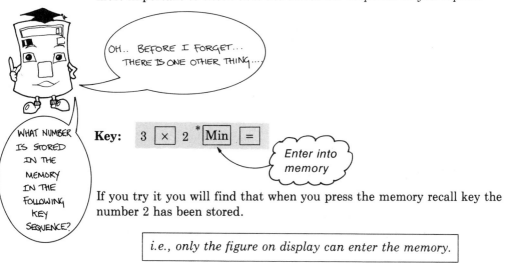

OH.. BEFORE I FORGET...
THERE IS ONE OTHER THING...

WHAT NUMBER IS STORED IN THE MEMORY IN THE FOLLOWING KEY SEQUENCE?

Key: 3 $\boxed{\times}$ 2 *$\boxed{\text{Min}}$ $\boxed{=}$

Enter into memory

If you try it you will find that when you press the memory recall key the
number 2 has been stored.

     i.e., only the figure on display can enter the memory.

SEE SECTION 5C
FOR AN APPLICATION.

---

*Use key appropriate to your calculator.

4B A perfect problem?

Clear your calculator memory at the start of each of these questions.

1. Check which of the numbers listed below are factors of 496. Each time you find a factor add it to the contents of the memory. When you have checked all of the numbers display the contents of the memory:

$$1, 2, 3, 4, 6, 8, 12, 16, 31, 32, 62, 64, 124, 248.$$

Any number which is equal to the sum of its proper divisors is called a 'perfect' number.

Note: 1 is included as a proper divisor but the number itself is not.

2. Check that 6 and 28 are perfect numbers.

4C Memory in practice

A situation that often arises is that a particular number may appear over and over again within a calculation. In such cases it is convenient to store the number in the memory and recall it at the appropriate times.

Make use of the calculator memory to find the value of y for the given values of x.

1. $y = x^2 - 3x + 2$
   a) $x = 2.73$ b) $x = 5.61$ c) $x = -3.92$

2. $y = 2x^2 - \dfrac{1}{x} + 5$
   a) $x = 0.327$ b) $x = 1.85$ c) $x = -2.31$

3. $y = x^3 + 5x^2 - 2x + 3$
   a) $x = 0.471$ b) $x = 2.84$ c) $x = -1.72$

Consider the following examples.

$$x = \sqrt{84}, \quad y = x^3 \qquad \text{Find } x \text{ and } y \text{ to 3 s.f.}$$

$$x = 9.165\ldots \quad \text{(CALC)}$$

∴ $$x = 9.17 \ (3 \text{ s.f.})$$

To find y use the full value of x displayed on the calculator and *not* the rounded value.

giving $$y = 769.8\ldots \quad \text{(CALC)}$$

$$y = 770 \quad (3 \text{ s.f.})$$

Note: When rounded values are used in subsequent calculations rounding errors can build up and distort the solution. In this example we would have $9.17^3 = 771$ to 3 s.f.

Find the values of x and y to 3 s.f.

4. $x = \sqrt{73}$ $\quad y = x^3 - 3x$ $\qquad$ 6. $\quad x = \sqrt[3]{9}$ $\qquad y = 3x^2 + x - 5$

5. $x = \dfrac{1}{15}$ $\quad y = x^2 + 2x$ $\qquad$ 7. $\quad x = \dfrac{3.6 \times 5.7}{2.3}$ $\quad y = x^2 + x + \dfrac{1}{x}$

8. Find the value of **a)** y $\qquad$ **b)** $y + x$ to 3 s.f.,
   where $y = 2x^2 + 5$ and $x = 0.0187$ $\qquad$ (Store x in the memory.)

9. Find the value of **a)** y $\qquad$ **b)** $x^2 y$ to 3 s.f.,
   where $y = 26.3x - 12.8$ and $x = 6.473$

10. Find the value of **a)** y $\qquad$ **b)** $\dfrac{y}{x}$ to 3 s.f.,
    where $y = \left(\dfrac{x}{4.9} + 12\right)^2$ and $x = 0.2418$

*11. In Section 3H a sequence of instructions was given that produced an approximation to the value of π.

   The key sequence† below provides a more efficient method which may be used to calculate π to a high degree of accuracy

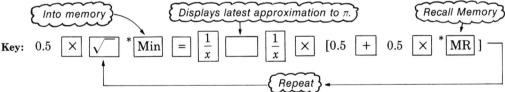

   Carry out the given key sequence until two consecutive approximations to π are the same. Write down the sequence of approximations produced.

*Use keys appropriate to your calculator. See Section 4A.
†The sequence is based on the fact that $2/\pi$ can be expressed as an infinite product

$$\frac{2}{\pi} = \sqrt{\frac{1}{2}} \cdot \sqrt{\frac{1}{2} + \frac{1}{2}\sqrt{\frac{1}{2}}} \cdot \sqrt{\frac{1}{2} + \frac{1}{2}\sqrt{\frac{1}{2} + \frac{1}{2}\sqrt{\frac{1}{2}}}} \cdots$$

As discovered by Francois Viete in 1579.

5 PERCENTAGES

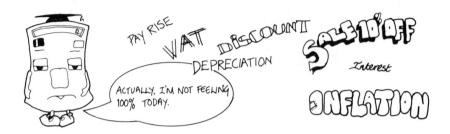

Many calculators are fitted with % or △% keys. Unfortunately there are so many variations in the way that these keys are used that it is not practical to consider all of the possibilities here.

In many of the exercises that follow, key sequences are given which do not make use of the % keys and which consequently should work on any machine. In any case you are likely to gain more in terms of *understanding percentages* by using the methods shown than by using the specialised keys.

5A From fractions to percentages

EXAMPLES:

(i) What is $\frac{5}{8}$ expressed as a percentage?

$\frac{5}{8} \times 100\%$ **Key:**   5 ÷ 8 × 100 =

$= 62.5\%$ (CALC)

(ii) Express 27.8 as a percentage of 41.32.

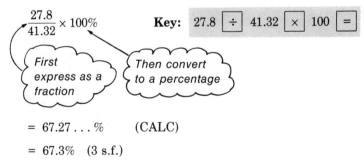

$\frac{27.8}{41.32} \times 100\%$ **Key:**   27.8 ÷ 41.32 × 100 =

First express as a fraction   *Then convert to a percentage*

$= 67.27\ldots\%$ (CALC)

$= 67.3\%$ (3 s.f.)

Write as percentages correct to 3 s.f.

1. $\dfrac{3}{8}$ 6. $\dfrac{2.65}{73.9}$

2. $\dfrac{4}{9}$ 7. $\dfrac{4.62}{5.31}$

3. $\dfrac{7}{15}$ 8. $\dfrac{173}{129}$

4. $\dfrac{23}{30}$ 9. $\dfrac{147}{96.2}$

5. $\dfrac{18.7}{43.2}$ 10. $\dfrac{107.3}{86.5}$

In each of the following, express the first quantity as a percentage of the second to 3 s.f.

11. 15, 37   16. 23.9 kg, 18.2 kg
12. 29, 18   17. 34 cm, 1.92 m
13. 63.5, 21.8   18. 83p, £2.61
14. 84 m, 123 m   19. 18 in, 3 ft
15. £27.60, £38   20. 57 lb, 3 cwt

5B   Percentages of an amount

EXAMPLE: 15% of 12.9 kg means $\dfrac{15}{100} \times 12.9$ kg

$= 1.935$ kg   (CALC)

Key: $15 \; \boxed{\div} \; 100 \; \boxed{\times} \; 12.9 \; \boxed{=}$

Evaluate exactly:

1. 15% of £83   6. 0.7% of 92 kg
2. 8% of £26   7. 14.2% of 50 cm
3. 16% of £172   8. 120% of £75
4. 23% of 57 m   9. 117.8% of 7530 m^2
5. 8.7% of 43 kg   10. 200% of £82.43

Calculate to the nearest penny:

11. 15% of £32.43   14. $12\frac{1}{2}$% of £18.57
12. 17% of £94.36
13. 8.6% of £6841.57   15. $33\frac{1}{3}$% of £51.62

5C Increasing by a percentage

EXAMPLE: Increase £43.89 by 27%

Method 1: One approach is to calculate 27% of £43.89 as in section 5B and then to add on £43.89 making use of the memory:

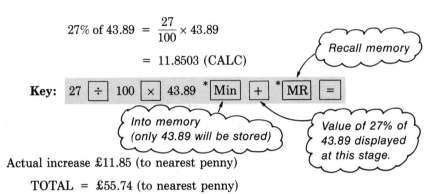

$$27\% \text{ of } 43.89 = \frac{27}{100} \times 43.89$$

$$= 11.8503 \text{ (CALC)}$$

Recall memory

Key: 27 ÷ 100 × 43.89 *Min + *MR =

Into memory (only 43.89 will be stored)

Value of 27% of 43.89 displayed at this stage.

Actual increase £11.85 (to nearest penny)

TOTAL = £55.74 (to nearest penny)

> (i) *Method 1* is the most useful when the *actual increase* is required as well as the final total.
> (ii) The key sequence may be slightly shortened by entering 27% as 0.27 directly rather than as 27 ÷ 100.

Method 2: £43.89 may be regarded as 100% of itself and so increasing £43.89 by 27% is equivalent to calculating 127% of £43.89

$$127\% \text{ of } 43.89 = \frac{127}{100} \times 43.89 \quad \textbf{Key: } \boxed{127} \boxed{÷} \boxed{100} \boxed{\times} \boxed{43.89} \boxed{=}$$

$$= 55.7403 \text{ (CALC)}$$

TOTAL = £55.74 (to nearest penny)

YOU MAY NEED SOMETHING DIFFERENT HERE SEE SECTION 1.E.

Although the actual increase is not displayed using *Method 2* the method has a particular advantage when several figures are to be increased by the same percentage.

Using *Method 2* the increase was effected by multiplying by 127 ÷ 100 i.e. 1.27.

This same factor can be used to increase any figure by 27% and so when the process is to be repeated we simply use the constant multiplier facility.

If the key sequence given for *Method 2* is extended to . . .

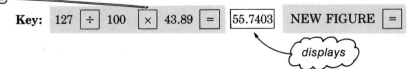

Key: 127 ÷ 100 × 43.89 = 55.7403 NEW FIGURE =

displays

---

* Use appropriate key for your calculator. See Section 4A.

... then the 'new figure' will also be increased by 27% as will any subsequent amounts that are entered and followed by $\boxed{=}$

1. Using *Method 1* increase the given values by the corresponding percentages stating the actual increase in each case. (Answers to 2 d.p.).

   a) £38, 25%
   b) £49.30, 16%
   c) 86 kg, 43%
   d) 57.03 m, 9.81%
   e) 27.4 litres, 12%

   f) 47.2 cm^3, $8\frac{1}{2}$%
   g) 0.26 volts, 4.6%
   h) £87.65, 124%
   i) 4.82 kg, 216%
   j) 58.90 m^2, 98.7%

2. Using *Method 2* add 15% VAT to each of the following:

   a) £2
   b) £5.30
   c) £96.57
   d) £18.23
   e) £31.51

   f) £87.50
   g) . £217.83
   h) 97p
   i) £4.05
   j) £768.54

3. Using the method of your choice increase the following amounts by the percentage shown giving your answers to the nearest penny:

   a) £23.42, 15%
   b) £16.81, 12%
   c) £123.41, 30%
   d) £97.63, 4%
   e) £31.62, 87%

   f) £2.72, 100%
   g) £5.29, 123%
   h) £7.94, 162%
   i) £3125, 8.7%
   j) £11 436, 2.8%

5D Reducing by a percentage

EXAMPLE: Reduce £56.42 by 12%.

Method 1: 12% of $56.42 = \dfrac{12}{100} \times 56.42$

$$= 6.7704 \qquad \text{(CALC)}$$

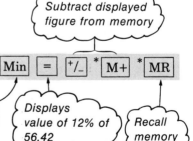

Key: 12 $\boxed{\div}$ 100 $\boxed{\times}$ 56.42 *$\boxed{\text{Min}}$ $\boxed{=}$ $\boxed{^+/_-}$ *$\boxed{\text{M+}}$ *$\boxed{\text{MR}}$

Subtract displayed figure from memory

Into memory

Displays value of 12% of 56.42

Recall memory

REDUCTION = £6.77 (to nearest penny)

Net amount = £49.65 (to nearest penny)

* Use key appropriate to your calculator. See Section 4A.

Method 2: Reducing £56.42 by 12% is equivalent to calculating 88% of £56.42 (i.e. 100% − 12%).

$$88\% \text{ of } 56.42 = \frac{88}{100} \times 56.42$$

Key: $\boxed{88} \boxed{\div} \boxed{100} \boxed{\times} \boxed{56.42} \boxed{=}$

$$49.6496 \qquad \text{(CALC)}$$

Net amount = £49.65 (to nearest penny)

> The methods shown here have the corresponding advantages to those shown in Section 5C.

1. Reduce the given values by the corresponding percentages stating the actual reduction in each case. (Answers to 2 d.p.)

   a) £65, 25%

   b) £18.32, 12%

   c) 9.86 litres, 17%

   d) 186 kg, $8\frac{1}{2}\%$

   e) 369 cm^3, 43%

   f) 58 s, 3.2%

   g) 98.2 m, 53%

   h) 48.6 lb, 16%

   i) 479 km, 7.6%

   j) 164.8°, $4\frac{3}{4}\%$

2. In a sale all prices are to be reduced by 7%. Calculate the sale price for items originally marked as follows:

   a) £64.49

   b) £32.65

   c) £12.82

   d) £4.99

   e) £17.31

   f) £125.80

   g) £46.34

   h) £252.16

   i) £341.90

   j) £416.27

5E To express an increase/decrease as a percentage

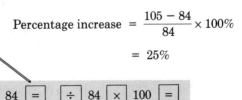

NOTE HOW THE "=" SIGN HAS BEEN USED SO THAT THE SUBTRACTION IS CARRIED OUT FIRST.

EXAMPLE 1: By what percentage must 84 be increased to make 105?

Method: Express the *increase* as a fraction of the original number and multiply by 100.

$$\text{Percentage increase} = \frac{105 - 84}{84} \times 100\%$$

$$= 25\%$$

Key: $\boxed{105} \boxed{-} \boxed{84} \boxed{=} \boxed{\div} \boxed{84} \boxed{\times} \boxed{100} \boxed{=}$

EXAMPLE 2: By what percentage must 75 be reduced to make 63?

Method: Express the *decrease* as a fraction of the original number and multiply by 100.

$$\text{Percentage reduction } = \frac{75 - 63}{75} \times 100\%$$

$$= 16\% \text{ (CALC)}$$

Key: 75 $\boxed{-}$ 63 $\boxed{=}$ $\boxed{\div}$ 75 $\boxed{\times}$ 100 $\boxed{=}$

For each of the pairs of numbers below, calculate the percentage by which the first must be increased/decreased to make the second. Give your answer to 3 s.f.

1. 60, 90
2. 53, 67
3. 29, 36
4. 83, 92
5. 16, 18.2

6. 53, 48
7. 76, 53
8. 152, 141
9. 38, 82
10. 47.53, 21.72

The methods of this section may also be used to express profit or loss as a percentage and to calculate percentage error.

11. The figures given below indicate respectively the cost price and selling price of some articles. In each case express the profit or loss as a percentage of the cost price to 3 s.f.
    a) £83.72, £95.61
    b) £247.83, £279.20
    c) £853.40, £684.70
    d) £5672, £4175
    e) £1476.93, £4387.62
    f) £1075.80, £350

*12. The sides of a rectangle are measured to the nearest millimetre as 3.2 cm and 1.8 cm. These figures are then used to calculate the area of the rectangle. Find the maximum percentage error in the result.

5F Reverse percentages

EXAMPLE: The price of an article is given as £26.45 which includes VAT at 15%. What was the price of the article before VAT was added?

We know from Section 5C that VAT could have been added to the original price by multiplying it by 115 ÷ 100, i.e. 1.15

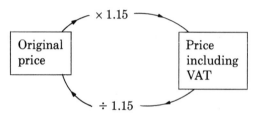

We see from the diagram that the problem may be solved by effectively 'going into reverse' and *dividing* the inclusive price by 1.15.

Key: 26.45 ÷ 1.15 =

This tells us that the original price was £23.

1. Find the original prices before VAT at 15% was added to make these totals:

   a) £47.15   **f)** £135.24
   b) £98.90   **g)** £122.13
   c) £31.51   **h)** £32.87
   d) £21.39   **i)** £417.43
   e) £79.12   **j)** £386.52

2. In each of the following an unknown value has been increased by the percentage shown to make the given amount.

   Calculate the unknown value in each case correct to the nearest whole number.

   a) 10% 88   **c)** 16% 92   **e)** 9% 165
   b) 20% 24   **d)** 7% 53   **f)** 12% 216

g) 23% 517

i) 12.7% 96

h) 1.6% 387

j) 124% 225

3. The total price of an article, including VAT at 15%, is given as:

    a) £74.30

    d) £1.82

    b) £81.60

    e) 96p

    c) £279.47

In each case find the amount of VAT included in the price.
Answers to be given to the nearest penny.

Note: The technique described in this section provides us with a method
for *checking our answers* to questions such as those in Sections 5C
and 5D.

e.g. if the key sequence given for Method 1 of Section 5C is followed by

$$\boxed{\div}\ \ 1.27\ \ \boxed{=}$$

then the original figure, i.e. 43.89, should be displayed.

5G Converting marks to percentages

EXAMPLE: In a test marked out of 47 a pupil obtained a mark of 36.
Convert the mark to a percentage.

36 out of 47 can be written as $\dfrac{36}{47}$ and to convert it to a percentage we
multiply by 100.

Key: 36 $\boxed{\div}$ 47 $\boxed{\times}$ 100 $\boxed{=}$

Verify on your calculator that the same result is obtained with the following key sequence.

Key: 100 $\boxed{\div}$ 47 $\boxed{\times}$ 36 $\boxed{=}$

The advantage of this sequence is that we can again make use of the
constant multiplier using the factor $\dfrac{100}{47}$ to convert any given mark to a
percentage.

1. Ten pupils obtained the following marks in a test marked out of 47. Convert the marks to whole number percentages and find the average percentage as efficiently as possible.

   a) 39   f) 43
   b) 12   g) 28
   c) 15   h) 16
   d) 26   i) 3
   e) 32   j) 21

2. Repeat question 1 for a test marked out of 52.

3. The following pairs of numbers represent the marks obtained on the two sections of an examination paper marked out of a total of 147.

   Find the percentage scored in each case.

   a) 63, 58   f) 37, 39
   b) 42, 37   g) 58, 67
   c) 59, 36   h) 49, 54
   d) 46, 48   i) 68, 73
   e) 72, 69

   You will probably find it helpful to store the conversion factor in the calculator memory.

   Questions on simple interest and compound interest will be found in Chapter 8.

6 STANDARD FORM

DID YOU KNOW THAT THERE ARE ABOUT 300,000,000,000,000,000,000 ATOMS IN A PINHEAD?

6A What is standard form?

Very large and very small numbers occur quite naturally in some problems. The use of standard form or scientific notation, as it is sometimes called, enables us to write such numbers much more concisely than in the normal decimal notation.

Indeed without such a notation calculators would be much more limited in the range of numbers that they could handle.

In standard form a number is written as

$$A \times 10^n$$

Where $1 \leqslant A < 10$ and n is a whole number.

For large numbers n is *positive* and for small numbers (less than unity) n is *negative*.

The variable n may be regarded as the number of places that the decimal point must be moved from its position in 'A' to convert back to normal decimal notation regarding movement to the *right* as positive.

Some examples should help . . .

$$470\,000 = 4.7 \times 10^5$$

Between 1 and 10

Original position of point 5 places further to the right

$$0.000\,672 = 6.72 \times 10^{-4}$$

Between 1 and 10

Original position of point 4 places further to the left

6B Entering standard form on the calculator

On most calculators standard form is entered by using the EXP key as shown in the key sequences below. However, on some calculators the key is labelled EE.

We know for example that $470\,000 \div 100 = 4700$

To verify this on the calculator using standard form

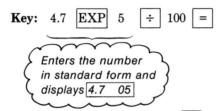

Key: 4.7 EXP 5 ÷ 100 =

Enters the number in standard form and displays 4.7 05

You may find on pressing the ÷ key that the calculator reverts to decimal notation (i.e. 470 000) since this will be well within its decimal range.

To verify that $0.000\,672 \times 10\,000 = 6.72$ using standard form

Key: 6.72 EXP 4 +/− × 10000 =

Displays 6.72 −04

Evaluate the following expressions mentally and then check the results using standard form on your calculator.

1.	$830\,000 \div 100$	**6.**	$0.000\,26 \times 10\,000$
2.	$9\,670\,000 \div 10\,000$	**7.**	$0.008\,63 \times 1000$
3.	$3\,410\,000 \div 100\,000$	**8.**	$0.004\,72 \times 100$
4.	$24\,000 \times 100$	**9.**	$0.000\,087 \div 10$
5.	5700×1000	**10.**	$0.000\,36 \div 100$

6C Reading standard form from the display

When the result of a calculation is outside the normal decimal range of the calculator display it will automatically convert the number to standard form.

Evaluate the following expressions on the calculator. Write the answers in standard form and then convert to decimal notation.

1.	$560\,000 \times 1000$	**4.**	$(2.86 \times 10^5) \times 20\,000$
2.	$273\,000 \times 1000$	**5.**	$(3.0 \times 10^7) \times 500$
3.	$5\,240\,000 \times 1000$	**6.**	$0.000\,032 \div 1000$

7. $0.000\ 008\ 6 \div 400$

9. $\dfrac{1}{50\ 000\ 000}$

8. $26.4 \div (4.0 \times 10^{1})$

10. $\dfrac{1}{2.5 \times 10^{9}}$

6D Further calculations involving standard form

Evaluate using the calculator and leave your answers in the most convenient form correct to 3 s.f.

1. $360\ 000 \times 71\ 000$

2. $8.72 \times 10^{5} \times 1000$

3. $\dfrac{5.61 \times 10^{12}}{100}$

4. $\dfrac{2.63 \times 10^{9}}{5.89 \times 10^{4}}$

5. $\dfrac{9.872 \times 10^{11}}{7.31 \times 10^{6}}$

6. $3.82 \times 10^{5} + 1.493 \times 10^{7}$

7. $8.73 \times 10^{7} - 9.6 \times 10^{4}$

8. $2.73 \times 10^{8} + 6.72 \times 10^{5} - 1.87 \times 10^{9}$

9. $\dfrac{1}{5.73 \times 10^{8}}$

10. $\dfrac{1}{2.64 \times 10^{6}}$

11. $8.31 \times 10^{-7} \times 2.4 \times 10^{3}$

12. $2.15 \times 10^{-3} \times 9.84 \times 10^{-6}$

13. $3700 \div (1.59 \times 10^{9})$

14. $(3.82 \times 10^{5})^{2}$

15. $\sqrt{4.72 \times 10^{-9}}$

16. $(4.61 \times 10^{-3})^{2}$

17. $\dfrac{1}{5.37 \times 10^{4}} + \dfrac{1}{8.13 \times 10^{5}}$

18. $\dfrac{1}{0.000\ 000\ 056\ 7}$

19. $\dfrac{1}{869\ 400\ 000}$

20. $\sqrt{4\ 926\ 000\ 000}$

6E That's torn it!

If you were given a large sheet of paper approximately 0.1 mm thick how many times do you think you could tear it in half if after each tearing all of the pieces were collected together?

A realistic answer might be somewhere between 5 and 8 times.

After each tearing the number of pieces of paper is doubled and so after 8 tearings the number of pieces is $2^{8} = 256$ which makes the height of the pile 2.56 cm.

On the assumption that the process could be repeated 50 times calculate the height of the pile of paper at the end.

YOU MIGHT BE SURPRISED BY THE RESULT!

PUT IT THIS WAY.... GIVE YOUR ANSWER IN KM... LOTS OF THEM!

7 TRIGONOMETRY

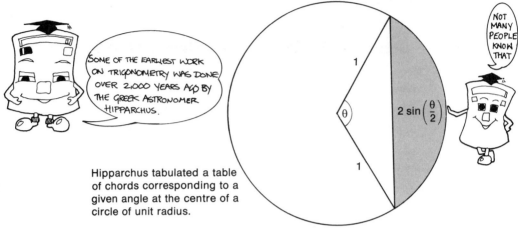

Hipparchus tabulated a table of chords corresponding to a given angle at the centre of a circle of unit radius.

7A Finding sines, cosines and tangents

EXAMPLE: Find the value of sin 28.6° to 4 s.f.

Key: 28.6° [SIN]

Giving $\qquad$ sin 28.6° = 0.478 691 8 = 0.4787 (to 4 s.f.)

Note: 1. The angle must be entered FIRST followed by the trig. function, i.e. the OPPOSITE way round to the way it is ALWAYS WRITTEN.

2. There is no need to press [=]

Answers to questions 1–7 may be given exactly. Give the value of the remaining expressions to 4 s.f.

1.	sin 30°	11.	tan 83°
2.	cos 60°	12.	cos 16.8°
3.	sin 90°	13.	cos 51.7°
4.	cos 0°	14.	sin 41.3°
5.	tan 0°	15.	sin 27.9°
6.	tan 45°	16.	tan 58.2°
7.	cos 90°	17.	cos 0.4°
8.	sin 38°	18.	tan 89.9°
9.	sin 76°	19.	tan 89.999°
10.	cos 20°	20.	tan 90°

7B Finding acute angles

EXAMPLE: Solve $\sin x = 0.4382$ where x is an *acute* angle.

Key: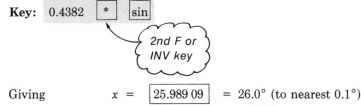

Giving $\qquad x = \boxed{25.989\ 09} = 26.0°$ (to nearest $0.1°$)

Once again there is no need to press the $\boxed{=}$ **key for the value to be displayed.**

Find the acute angle x in each of the following correct to the nearest $0.1°$.

1. $\sin x = 0.3721$

2. $\cos x = 0.7452$

3. $\sin x = 0.1873$

4. $\tan x = 0.8674$

5. $\tan x = 3.641$

6. $\sin x = \dfrac{5}{8}$

7. $\cos x = \dfrac{4}{7}$

8. $\tan x = \dfrac{11}{15}$

9. $\cos x = \dfrac{16.9}{25.6}$

10. $\sin x = \dfrac{6.34}{12.7}$

11. $\tan x = \dfrac{87.2}{36.9}$

12. $\sin x = \dfrac{572}{861}$

13. $\tan x = \sqrt{3}$

14. $\cos x = \dfrac{\sqrt{3}}{2}$

15. $\cos x = \dfrac{1}{\sqrt{2}}$

In the remaining questions you will first have to choose the appropriate ratio. The following definitions apply in any right-angled triangle.

$$\textbf{S}\text{ine (angle)} = \frac{\textbf{O}\text{pposite side}}{\textbf{H}\text{ypotenuse}} \qquad \textbf{C}\text{osine (angle)} = \frac{\textbf{A}\text{djacent side}}{\textbf{H}\text{ypotenuse}}$$

$$\text{and } \textbf{T}\text{angent (angle)} = \frac{\textbf{O}\text{pposite side}}{\textbf{A}\text{djacent side}}$$

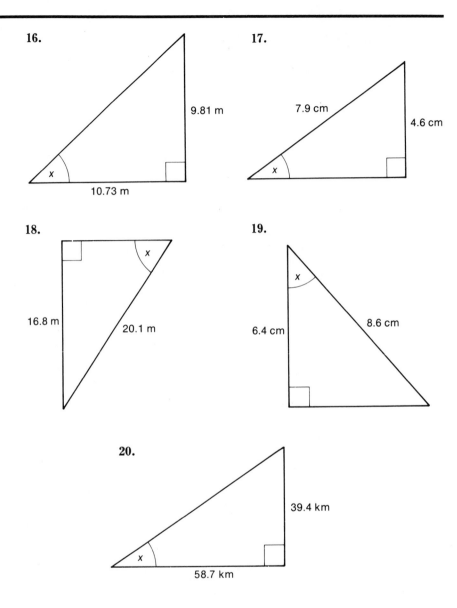

16.

9.81 m

10.73 m

x

17.

7.9 cm

4.6 cm

x

18.

16.8 m

20.1 m

x

19.

x

6.4 cm

8.6 cm

20.

39.4 km

58.7 km

x

*7C Working with obtuse angles

Find to 4 s.f. the trigonometric functions of the following:

1.   sin 125°
2.   cos 153°
3.   sin 98.2°
4.   tan 161°
5.   tan 107.5°

6.   cos 112.6°
7.   sin 172.4°
8.   cos 163.8°
9.   tan 90.01°
10.   tan 90.001°

EXAMPLES : Solve for x

        a) $\cos x = -0.8672$

        b) $\tan x = -1.246$

        c) $\sin x = 0.4319$

to the nearest $0.1°$ where in each case x is *obtuse*.

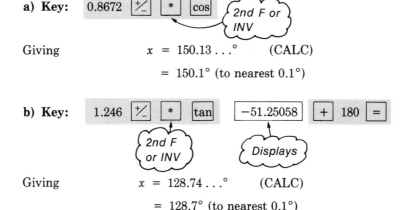

a) Key: 0.8672 ⊥ * cos (2nd F or INV)

Giving $x = 150.13\ldots°$ (CALC)

                           $= 150.1°$ (to nearest $0.1°$)

b) Key: 1.246 ⊥ * tan −51.25058 + 180 =

                       (2nd F or INV)   (Displays)

Giving $x = 128.74\ldots°$ (CALC)

                           $= 128.7°$ (to nearest $0.1°$)

Note: The original angle displayed, i.e. $-51.250\,58°$ is a solution to the equation but is not an OBTUSE angle. In general $\tan(180° + x) = \tan x$ and so a solution in the right range was found by adding on $180°$.

You can check the solution

Just press the tan key at the end of the sequence above and the original entry, i.e. -1.246 should be displayed, though some calculators may include a very slight rounding error (see Section 3B).

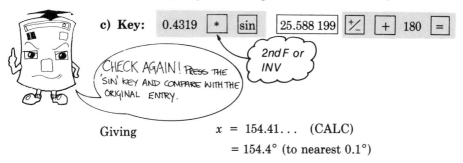

c) Key: 0.4319 * sin 25.588 199 ⊥ + 180 =

CHECK AGAIN! PRESS THE 'SIN' KEY AND COMPARE WITH THE ORIGINAL ENTRY.   (2nd F or INV)

Giving $x = 154.41\ldots$ (CALC)

                           $= 154.4°$ (to nearest $0.1°$)

Note: **Again the original angle displayed is a solution in the wrong range.**

            In general $\sin(180° - x) = \sin x$ and so a solution in the right range was found by subtracting the displayed value from $180°$. The simplest way to achieve this was to change the sign of the displayed angle and add 180.

Find the obtuse angles x to the nearest $0.1°$ such that:

11. $\cos x = -0.7342$ 16. $\tan x = -0.5714$

12. $\cos x = -0.1478$ 17. $\tan x = -1.835$

13. $\cos x = -0.6543$ 18. $\sin x = 0.3617$

14. $\cos x = -0.5482$ 19. $\sin x = 0.9412$

15. $\tan x = -0.8137$ 20. $\sin x = 0.1413$

7D Calculation of sides in a right-angled triangle

To evaluate $16 \sin 52°$

Key: $\boxed{16}$ $\boxed{\times}$ $\boxed{52}$ $\boxed{\sin}$ $\boxed{=}$

Giving $12.60 \ldots$ (CALC) $= 12.6$ (to 3 s.f.)

Note: When the $\boxed{\sin}$ key is pressed, the value displayed is 0.788 010 7,
i.e. sin 52°. Multiplication by the 16 is not carried out until the
$\boxed{=}$ key is pressed.

> Evaluation of a trig. function has *priority* over $+$, $-$, $\times$ and $\div$

Calculate to 3 s.f.

1. $10 \sin 43°$ 6. $24.6 \sin 82.1°$

2. $8.6 \cos 29°$ 7. $65.1 \sin 32°$

3. $15.7 \tan 63.2°$ 8. $0.73 \cos 23.7°$

4. $12.8 \cos 76.4°$ 9. $\sqrt{3} \tan 75.1°$

5. $18 \tan 63.5°$ 10. $\sqrt{5} \cos 18.6°$

Find the value of x in each of the following.

11.

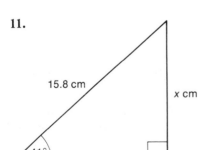

12.

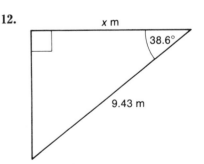

13.

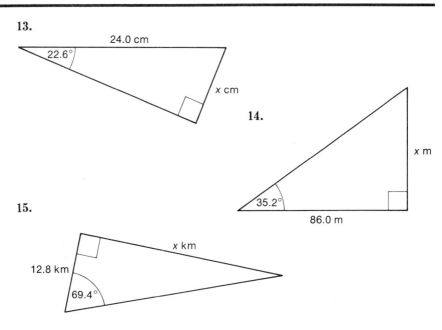

24.0 cm

22.6°

x cm

14.

x m

35.2°

86.0 m

15.

x km

12.8 km

69.4°

EXAMPLE: To calculate $\dfrac{16.1}{\cos 14.8°}$

Key: 16.1 ÷ 14.8 cos =

NOTICE THE PRIORITY OF 'COS' OVER '÷'.

Giving 16.65 ... (CALC) = 16.7 (3 s.f.)

Calculate to 3 s.f.

16. $\dfrac{34.8}{\cos 64.3°}$

17. $\dfrac{8.92}{\sin 24.1°}$

18. $\dfrac{183}{\cos 38.2°}$

19. $\dfrac{53.4}{\sin 76.2°}$

20. $\dfrac{3870}{\cos 54.6°}$

Find x:

21.

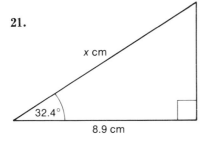

x cm

32.4°

8.9 cm

22.

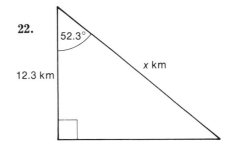

52.3°

x km

12.3 km

23.

24.

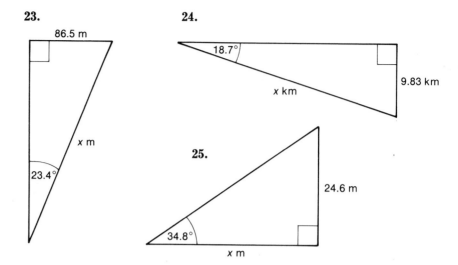

25.

26. The angle of elevation of the top of a tree from a point 12 m from its base is measured as 38°. Calculate the height of the tree to the nearest 0.5 m.

27. The angle of depression of a small boat when measured from a cliff top 60 m above the sea is found to be 18°. Calculate the distance of the boat from the foot of the cliff to the nearest 10 m.

28. A ladder 3 m long leans against a vertical wall, making an angle of 42° with the horizontal. Calculate the height of the top of the ladder above the ground to the nearest 0.1 m.

29. A ship sails at 12 knots on a bearing of 072° for $2\frac{1}{2}$ hours. How far has the ship sailed a) north b) east in that time?

30. Town Y lies on a bearing of 243° from town X and is 35 km further south. Find the direct distance from X to Y.

8 USE OF FORMULAE

Scientific calculators are particularly well suited to the substitution of given values into a formula. In this chapter a wide variety of applications of formulae at GCSE level will be considered.

Full key sequences will not be stated at this stage but hints and reminders of important points will still be given in addition to the necessary formulae – in many instances the formulae will require re-arrangement first.

NOTES FOR EXAMINATIONS:

1. Where a formula involves the use of π its value will be given in the question.
    Use this value rather then using the π key.

2. Make sure that your written solution includes the numerical expression that you have evaluated by calculator and that you write (CALC) to show that a calculator has been used. Failure to do this may mean that you *lose marks for method*.

3. Avoid using rounded values in subsequent calculations.

4. Always *check* your work in some way so that 'silly' answers are avoided.

    For example, make sure that the answer looks 'about right' in terms of size and that where necessary it has been rounded to a suitable level of accuracy.

8A The circle

1. The circumference of a circle is given by

$$C = 2\pi r \quad or \quad C = \pi d$$

Take $\pi = 3.142$ and calculate the missing values in the table below, correct to 3 s.f. All measurements are given in m.

	a)	b)	c)	d)	e)	f)	g)	h)	i)	j)
r	8.6	12.1	7.30	14.8						
d					6.40	0.70	9.52			
C								26.0	8.27	156

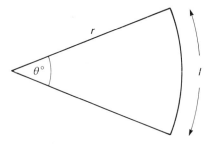

The length of arc, l, and the area of a sector, A, are given by

$$l = \frac{\theta}{360} \times 2\pi r = \frac{\theta \pi r}{180}$$

and

$$A = \frac{\theta}{360} \times \pi r^2 = \frac{\theta \pi r^2}{360}$$

respectively.

2. Calculate the missing values to 3 s.f. (Take $\pi = 3.142$)

						*	*	*	*	*
	a)	b)	c)	d)	e)	f)	g)	h)	i)	j)
r (cm)	12.8	31.7	125	86.0	56.2			14.8	23.6	
$\theta°$	135	74	270	55	124	58	240			36
l (cm)						36.9	76.2			
A (cm)^2								248	167	82.8

3.

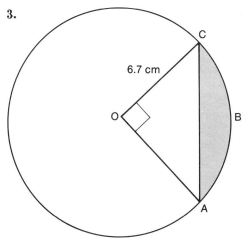

a) Find the area of the quadrant OABC

b) Calculate the area of △OAC

c) Hence find the area of the shaded segment.

Take $\pi = 3.142$

8B The sphere

The surface area of a sphere is given by

$$A = 4\pi r^2$$

and its volume is given by

$$V = \frac{4}{3}\pi r^3$$

1. Calculate the missing values from the table giving your answers to 3 s.f. Take $\pi = 3.142$.

	a)	b)	c)	d)	e)	f)	g)	h)	i)	j)
r (m)	5.80	0.42	0.81	1.76	2.43	18.2				
A (m²)							256	1.93		
V (m³)									18.9	0.246

DON'T FORGET THE AREA OF THE CIRCULAR BASE

*2. Calculate

a) the volume

b) the surface area

of a hemisphere of radius 8.7 cm giving your answer to 3 s.f. (Take $\pi = 3.142$)

*3. Two metal spheres of radii 8 cm and 7 cm are melted down and formed into a single sphere. Calculate the surface area and the volume of the new sphere to 3 s.f. (Take $\pi = 3.142$)

8C The cylinder

The surface area for a closed cylinder is given by $S = 2\pi r(r + h)$

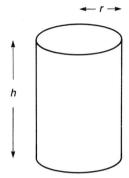

And the volume is $V = \pi r^2 h$

Note: The formula for the volume of a cylinder is a special case of a more general result for a figure with a *constant cross-section.*

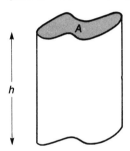

$V = Ah$

In the case of the cylinder $A = \pi r^2$ which is the area of the *circular* cross-section.

1. Calculate the missing values to 3 s.f. (Take $\pi = 3.142$)

	a)	b)	c)	d)	e)
r (cm)	6.2	12.4	28.3	7.5	81.0
h (cm)	15.1	30.2	15.4	31.6	0.9
S (cm^2)					
V (cm^3)					

*2. A cylinder of volume 48.3 cm^3 is such that its radius and height are equal.

   Find **a)** the radius

   b) the surface area of the cylinder.

   Answers to 3 s.f. (Take $\pi = 3.142$)

3. The diagram shows the circular cross-section of a pipe of internal diameter 3.8 cm constructed of plastic which is 1 cm thick.

Calculate to 3 s.f. (Take $\pi = 3.142$)

a) the shaded area.

b) the volume of plastic contained in a section of pipe 12 m long. Give your answer in cm^3.

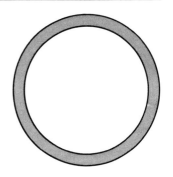

8D The cone

The total surface area of a cone is given by

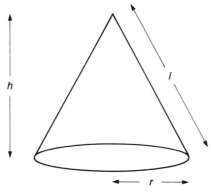

$$A = \pi r \, (r + l)$$

and the volume is

$$V = \tfrac{1}{3}\pi r^2 h$$

h is referred to as the height of the cone and l as the *slant* height. r is the radius of the circular base.

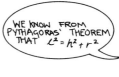

WE KNOW FROM PYTHAGORAS' THEOREM THAT $l^2 = h^2 + r^2$

1. Find the missing values to 3 s.f. (Take $\pi = 3.142$)

	a)	b)	c)	d)	e)
r (cm)	12.1	8.30	19.6	5.40	
h (cm)	16.2	24.0			12.4
l (cm)			37.1	16.7	
A (cm^2)					
V (cm^3)					478

2.

B. SMITH (BUILDER)

A builder wants to assess the quantity of sand that he has on site. The sand has been tipped from a wagon and has settled in the shape of a cone. He measures the slant height as 3.5 m and the perpendicular height as 1.6 m.

Take $\pi = 3.1$ and calculate the volume of sand to the nearest m³.

8E More areas and volumes

1.

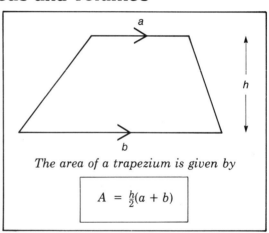

The area of a trapezium is given by

$$A = \frac{h}{2}(a + b)$$

33.33 m

0.7 m

3.2 m

The diagram shows the cross-section of a swimming pool viewed from the side.
Calculate to 3 s.f.

a) the area of cross-section

b) the volume of water in the pool when full given that it is 8.4 m wide

c) the mass of water that the pool can contain given that the mass of 1 m³ is 1000 kg. Give your answer in standard form.

2. Find the area of each of these triangles to 2 s.f.

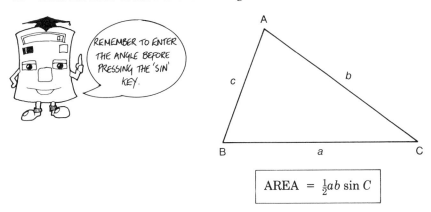

$$\text{AREA} = \tfrac{1}{2}ab \sin C$$

Note: The convention used in labelling the triangle is that the vertices are labelled with capital letters and the opposite sides are assigned the corresponding small letters.

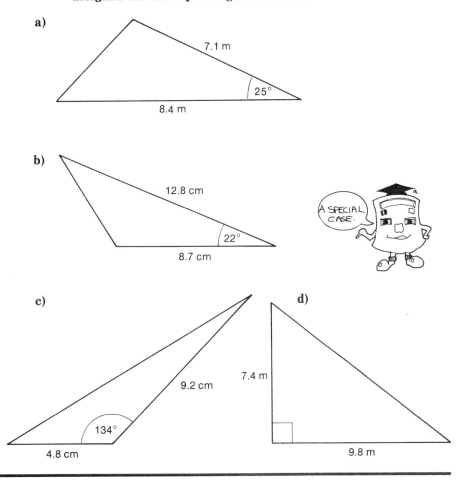

*3. In each case find the area to 3 s.f.

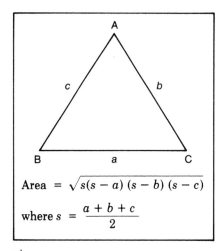

FIND S FIRST AND STORE IT IN THE MEMORY

Area $= \sqrt{s(s-a)(s-b)(s-c)}$

where $s = \dfrac{a+b+c}{2}$

a)

4.2 cm

6.7 cm

8.3 cm

b)

9.2 cm

16.8 cm

22.3 cm

c)

5 cm

12 cm

13 cm

A SPECIAL CASE!

4. Find the volume of each of the triangular prisms below to 3 s.f.

a)

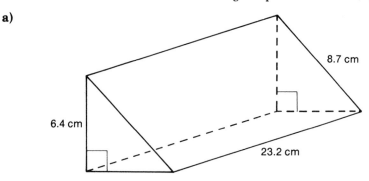

8.7 cm

6.4 cm

23.2 cm

b)

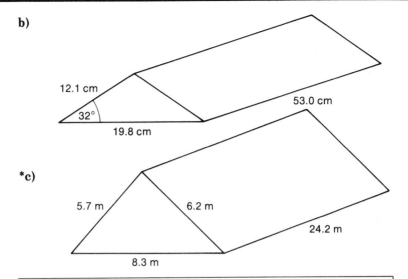

12.1 cm

32°

19.8 cm

53.0 cm

*c)

5.7 m

6.2 m

24.2 m

8.3 m

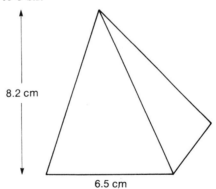

The volume of a pyramid $= \dfrac{1}{3}$ *base area* × *perpendicular height*

The volume of a cone, given earlier, is a special case of this result.

5. **a)** The diagram shows a square-based pyramid. Calculate its volume to 3 s.f.

8.2 cm

6.5 cm

b) The tetrahedron shown has a volume of 48.2 cm³ find the area of △ ABC to 2 s.f.

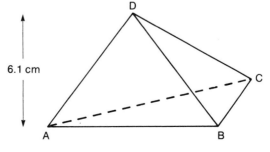

D

6.1 cm

C

A

B

8F The gradient of a line

Given that a straight line passing through points with co-ordinates
(x_1, y_1), (x_2, y_2) has a gradient given by

$$\frac{y_1 - y_2}{x_1 - x_2}$$

1. Find in each of the following the gradient of the straight line passing
    through the given pair of points.

    a) (8, 7), (5, 1)   **f)** (−1.8, 17.6), (4.2, 20.7)

    b) (−6, 5), (2, 9)   **g)** (4.7, 8.3), (12.9, 7.8)

    c) (−5, 3), (1, 6)   **h)** (19.2, −3.8), (27.6, −8.7)

    d) (2, 3), (5, −9)   **i)** (−9.4, −3.8), (6.1, 15.7)

    e) (3, −7), (−5, 3)

2. Find the gradient of each of the graphs drawn below and include the
    appropriate units. Give a possible interpretation of each graph and its
    gradient.

a)

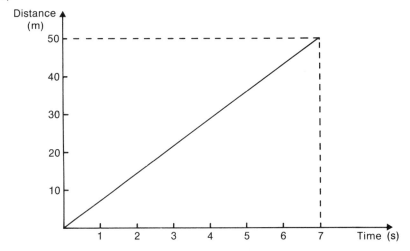

b)

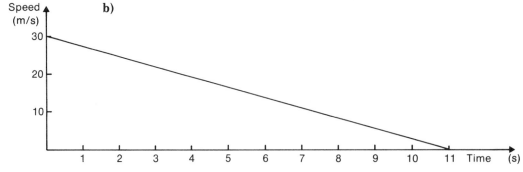

8G Simple interest

The *simple interest, I,* gained on a *principal* sum, *P*, invested at *R* % *rate* of interest per annum for time *T* years is given by

$$I = \frac{PRT}{100}$$ And the *amount A* is given by $$A = P + I$$

1. Calculate the missing values in the table:

	a)	b)	c)	d)	e)	f)	g)	h)
P	150	231.50	572.86	612.20		308.79	643.82	
R	8	$6\frac{3}{4}$	$9\frac{1}{2}$	$8\frac{7}{8}$	$11\frac{1}{4}$			
T	7	4	$2\frac{1}{2}$	$3\frac{5}{12}$	$2\frac{1}{3}$	$1\frac{3}{4}$	$2\frac{1}{12}$	$\frac{11}{12}$
I					87.52			37.55
A						341.62	761.43	361.55

Note: **a)** If you enter the mixed numbers by the method given in Section 1G then enclose the calculation in brackets.
For example . . . × (3 + 5 ÷ 12) × . . .

b) In Questions (**a**) to (**d**) it is helpful to store the value of *P* in the memory in order to calculate *A* when *I* has been found. Try and find similar short-cuts in the remaining questions.

8H Compound interest

If a principal sum, *P* is invested at *R* % per annum to gain *compound* interest then the amount *A* after *T* years is given by

$$A = P\left(1 + \frac{R}{100}\right)^T$$

STORE 'P' IN THE MEMORY AND SUBTRACT IT FROM 'A' TO FIND THE COMPOUND INTEREST

1. Find the amount and the compound interest for the given values of *P, R, T*.

	a)	b)	c)	d)	e)	f)
P	200	350	420	367.80	572.54	9760
R	8	9	$8\frac{1}{2}$	$9\frac{1}{4}$	$8\frac{3}{4}$	$11\frac{1}{8}$
T	5	3	4	4	$5\frac{1}{2}$	$7\frac{1}{3}$

$$P = \frac{A}{\left(1 + \dfrac{R}{100}\right)^T} = A\left(1 + \frac{R}{100}\right)^{-T}$$

2. Find the principal and the compound interest for each of the following values of A, T and R.

	a)	b)	c)	d)	e)	f)
A	387.52	512.96	409.23	638.50	816.53	5760.53
T	4	3	5	$4\frac{1}{2}$	$2\frac{1}{2}$	$4\frac{1}{2}$
R	6.4	$8\frac{1}{2}$	9	$9\frac{1}{4}$	$9\frac{1}{2}$	$10\frac{1}{4}$

*8I The sine rule

To find a *side* use

$$\frac{a}{\sin A} = \frac{b}{\sin B} = \frac{c}{\sin C}$$

To find an *angle* use

$$\frac{\sin A}{a} = \frac{\sin B}{b} = \frac{\sin C}{c}$$

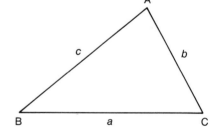

Note: The convention used in labelling the triangle is as explained in section 8E. The point of using this convention is that the rule is then easy to learn and to apply.

1. Calculate to 3 s.f.

a) $\dfrac{6.3 \sin 42°}{\sin 57°}$

b) $\dfrac{8.7 \sin 61°}{\sin 38°}$

c) $\dfrac{2.7 \sin 52.3°}{\sin 61.4°}$

d) $\dfrac{8.93 \sin 76°}{\sin 29.6°}$

e) $\dfrac{25.1 \sin 39.6°}{\sin 120.3°}$

2. Find the lengths of the unknown sides in these triangles:

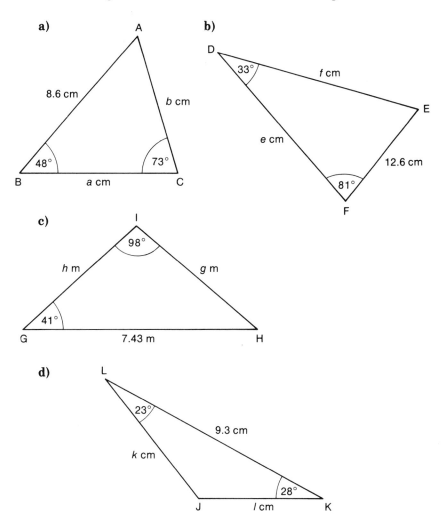

a)

b)

c)

d)

3. Find the *acute* angle θ such that:

a) $\sin \theta = \dfrac{5 \sin 28°}{7}$

b) $\sin \theta = \dfrac{8.4 \sin 64°}{11.3}$

c) $\sin \theta = \dfrac{7.2 \sin 36.2°}{5.8}$

d) $\sin \theta = \dfrac{12.8 \sin 120°}{17.9}$

e) $\sin \theta = \dfrac{8.34 \sin 136.2°}{25.7}$

4. Find the unknown angle θ in each of these triangles. In each case θ is acute.

a)

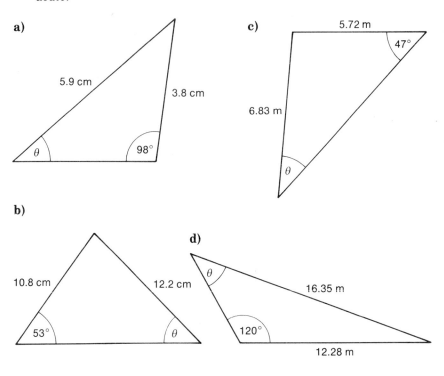

5.9 cm

3.8 cm

θ

98°

c)

5.72 m

47°

6.83 m

θ

b)

10.8 cm

12.2 cm

53°

θ

d)

θ

16.35 m

120°

12.28 m

*8J The cosine rule

To find a *side* use

$$a^2 = b^2 + c^2 - 2bc\cos A$$

with the usual convention for labelling the sides and vertices of a triangle.

To find an *angle* use

$$\cos A = \frac{b^2 + c^2 - a^2}{2bc}$$

1. Calculate to 3 s.f.
   a) $8.1^2 + 3.5^2 - 2 \times 8.1 \times 3.5 \cos 63°$
   b) $5.9^2 + 12.7^2 - 2 \times 5.9 \times 12.7 \cos 32°$
   c) $14.6^2 + 11.5^2 - 2 \times 14.6 \times 11.5 \cos 130°$
   d) $\sqrt{4.7^2 + 2.6^2 - 2 \times 4.7 \times 2.6 \cos 37°}$
   e) $\sqrt{9.6^2 + 12.8^2 - 2 \times 9.6 \times 12.8 \cos 121°}$

REMEMBER TO PRESS '=' BEFORE FINDING THE $\sqrt{}$

2. Find the length of the unknown side in each case to 3 s.f.

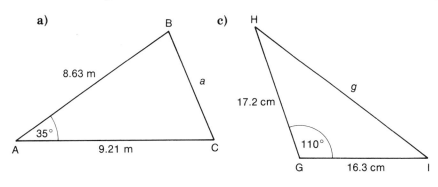

a)

8.63 m · 35° · B · a · 9.21 m · C · A

c) H · 17.2 cm · g · 110° · G · 16.3 cm · I

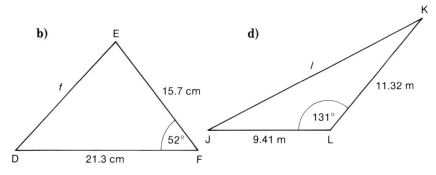

b) E · f · 15.7 cm · 52° · D · 21.3 cm · F · J

d) K · l · 11.32 m · 131° · 9.41 m · L

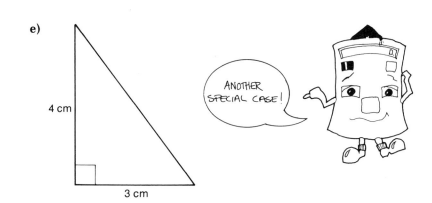

e)

4 cm

3 cm

ANOTHER SPECIAL CASE!

3. Find the angle θ such that $0° \leqslant \theta \leqslant 180°$ and

a) $\cos \theta = \dfrac{5^2 + 7^2 - 4^2}{2 \times 5 \times 7}$

b) $\cos \theta = \dfrac{8.1^2 + 6.3^2 - 7.5^2}{2 \times 8.1 \times 6.3}$

c) $\cos \theta = \dfrac{6.8^2 + 9.2^2 - 11.4^2}{2 \times 6.8 \times 9.2}$

d) $\cos \theta = \dfrac{5.3^2 + 7.1^2 - 11.8^2}{2 \times 5.3 \times 7.1}$

e) $\cos \theta = \dfrac{12.6^2 + 8.7^2 - 17.3^2}{2 \times 12.6 \times 8.7}$

4. Find the unknown angle θ in each of these triangles:

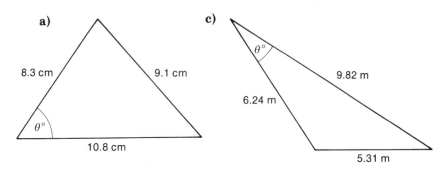

a)

8.3 cm   9.1 cm

$\theta°$

10.8 cm

c)

$\theta°$

6.24 m

9.82 m

5.31 m

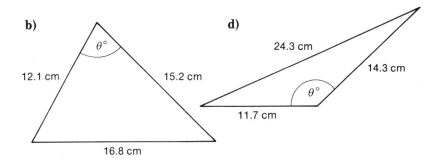

b)

$\theta°$

12.1 cm   15.2 cm

16.8 cm

d)

24.3 cm

14.3 cm

$\theta°$

11.7 cm

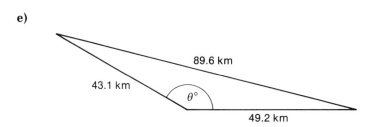

e)

89.6 km

43.1 km

$\theta°$

49.2 km

*8K The quadratic formula

If $ax^2 + bx + c = 0$

Then $x = \dfrac{-b \pm \sqrt{b^2 - 4ac}}{2a}$

Use the formula to find solutions to the following equations correct to 3 s.f.

1. $x^2 + 5x + 2 = 0$

2. $x^2 + 7x + 3 = 0$

3. $x^2 + 6x + 2 = 0$

4. $x^2 - 5x + 2 = 0$

5. $x^2 - 7x - 3 = 0$

6. $x^2 - 8x - 5 = 0$

7. $x^2 - 2x - 7 = 0$

8. $3x^2 + 6x - 5 = 0$

9. $2x^2 + 7x + 3 = 0$

10. $6.1x^2 - 3.5x - 2.9 = 0$

HINT-
STORE THE VALUE OF
$\sqrt{5^2 - 4 \times 1 \times 2}$
IN THE MEMORY.

*8L Iterative formulae

An iterative formula is fundamentally different from those studied elsewhere in the text. We need to have a rough idea of the final answer to start with and this value is substituted into the formula to produce a result that is more accurate than our original estimate. We then take our improved estimate, known as the first iteration, and substitute it into the *same formula* to produce the second iteration. The process is repeated until successive iterations are in agreement to the required level of accuracy.

For example the formula

$$x_{n+1} = \frac{1}{2}\left(x_n + \frac{a}{x_n}\right)$$

is an iterative formula for finding $\sqrt{a}$.

Basically the formula tells us how to calculate the $(n+1)$th iteration x_{n+1} (i.e. the new estimate) by substituting the nth iteration x_n (i.e. the present estimate) in the right-hand side of the equation.

The key sequence below illustrates how the formula may be used to calculate $\sqrt{3}$ taking 1.5 as the initial estimate.

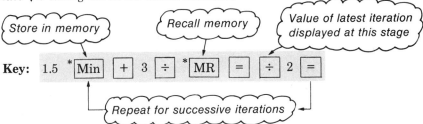

This sequence produces

$x_0 = 1.5$ $x_1 = 1.75$ $x_2 = 1.732\,142\,9$ $x_3 = 1.732\,050\,8$ $x_4 = 1.732\,050\,8$

Notice how the sequence has *converged* to the full accuracy of the calculator after only three iterations.

In Question 7 of Exercise 8K you were asked to solve the equation $x^2 - 2x - 7 = 0$ using the quadratic formula.

*Use key appropriate to your calculator. See Section 4A.

The two solutions work out as

$$3.828\ 427\ 1 \text{ and } -1.828\ 427\ 1$$

to the full accuracy of the calculator.

Use the iterative formula

$$x_{n+1} = \frac{x_n^2 + 7}{2x_n - 2}$$

taking the first estimate as 3 and calculate the first four iterations. The key sequence and the value of the iterations are given in the answers if you need them.

Now use the *same iterative formula* with a first estimate of -2 and you should find that the sequence this time converges to the other root with full accuracy in three iterations!

The point to be made here is that calculators not only make substitution into standard formulae easier but that they may actually make feasible a different approach to solving a problem. This is particularly important in situations where perhaps a standard formula doesn't exist.

In Sections 3H and 4C key sequences were given that could be used to calculate the value of π. The iteration formula

$$x_{n+1} = x_n - \tan x_n$$

provides us with another method of calculating this elusive number. The key sequence below takes 3 as the initial estimate.

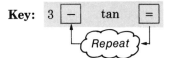

Note: The calculator must be set to work in radians for this key sequence.

Experiment by using the sequence with different initial estimates and comment on your findings.

There is much more to be said about iterative formulae – the various methods for finding them and why they work (and why they sometimes don't). Unfortunately a full treatment is beyond the scope of this text but you may like to know that the formulae used in this section were derived from the general Newton-Raphson formula.

To conclude with a true story

Just the other day I was approached by the Head of the RE Department who presented me with the following problem.

"Is there a method for dividing a circle into two segments so that the area of the minor segment is one-fifth of the area of the complete circle?"

I didn't enquire as to why this was of any importance but immediately took up the challenge and responded as follows:

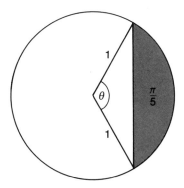

Considering a unit circle I defined the angle subtended by an appropriate chord at the centre of the circle to be θ radians.

This led to the equation

$$\frac{1}{2}\sin\theta + \frac{\pi}{5} = \frac{1}{2}\theta$$

$$\Rightarrow \quad \theta - \sin\theta - \frac{2\pi}{5} = 0$$

So far so good, but suddenly there was a problem. How could the equation be solved?

For a while I thought I might have to start the problem again and then I realised that the equation could be solved by iteration, using the formula

$$\theta_{n+1} = \theta_n - \frac{\theta_n - \sin\theta_n - \dfrac{2\pi}{5}}{1 - \cos\theta_n}$$

which is again based on the Newton-Raphson result.

If you would like to use the formula to find θ remember to set your calculator to work in radians. A key sequence is given in the answers if you need it.

Coincidence? Once θ is found the length of an appropriate chord is found by calculating $2\sin\left(\dfrac{\theta}{2}\right)$.

Now look at the illustration at the start of Chapter 7.

ANSWERS

P1
1. a) 0.37   b) 0.4
2. a) 0.47   b) 0.5
3. a) 0.53   b) 0.5
4. a) 0.61   b) 0.6
5. a) 0.30   b) 0.3
6. a) 2.47   b) 2.5
7. a) 8.60   b) 8.6
8. a) 12.75   b) 12.7
9. a) 116.85   b) 116.9
10. a) 7.04   b) 7.0
11. a) 19.06   b) 19.1
12. a) 16.05   b) 16.0
13. a) 0.84   b) 0.8
14. a) 84.00   b) 84.0
15. a) 147.40   b) 147.4

P2
1. £0.08
2. £0.83
3. £8.34
4. £0.72
5. £14.44
6. £722.02
7. £0.39
8. £39.22
9. £2.50
10. £7.84

P3
1. a) 5480   b) 5000
2. a) 81 700   b) 80 000
3. a) 17 500   b) 20 000
4. a) 25 900   b) 30 000
5. a) 6740   b) 7000
6. a) 17.4   b) 20
7. a) 6800   b) 7000
8. a) 12.5   b) 10
9. a) 0.785   b) 0.8
10. a) 0.0573   b) 0.06
11. a) 0.008 09   b) 0.008
12. a) 0.0801   b) 0.08
13. a) 0.0400   b) 0.04
14. a) 40.0   b) 40
15. a) 701 000   b) 700 000

P4
1. 600
2. 1600
3. 600
4. 300
5. 70
6. 150
7. 0.024
8. 0.56
9. 0.004
10. 0.0036
11. 20
12. 40
13. 5
14. 6.7
15. 5
16. 0.4
17. 0.06
18. 0.18
19. 2000
20. 1000

Note: These values are to be interpreted as 'rough answers' only. Accuracy to any number of significant figures is *not* implied.

P5
1. 7000
2. 5300
3. 43
4. 68
5. 106
6. 6.7
7. 19
8. 180
9. 440
10. 170
11. 550
12. 64
13. 130
14. 71 000
15. 540 000

P6 The incorrect statements are numbers:
2. Too big.   Must be less than $30 \times 50 = 1500$
3. Last figure must be zero
4. Too small.   Must be bigger than $3 \times 7 = 21$
5. Too big. $\dfrac{1}{2} \times 8.4 = 4.2$
8. Too big. $500 \div 25 = 20$
11. Must be less than 1
13. Too small. $60 + 8 - 20 = 48$
15. Too small. $50 + 8 - 0 = 58$
18. Too big. $13 + 3 + 1 + 2 = 19$
19. Too small.   Must be 3. (something)
21. Too big.   Must be less than $5^2 = 25$
23. Too big.   Must be less than 1
24. Too big.   Must be less than $\sqrt{3^2 + 4^2} = 5$
27. Too big.   Must be less than 15 since $\cos 76° < 1$
30. Too small.   Must be greater than 10 since $\sin 32° < 1$

P7 1. 2.4 or even 2.44. Although it is impossible to have 2.44 (or 2.4) children the extra figure would be useful for the purpose of comparison of results from different areas.

2. 78%. Rounding to the nearest whole number gives sufficient accuracy here.

3. 36 000 Taking into account the likely variation of stride length with different conditions any greater accuracy would be unreasonable.

4. 87°. Whole number accuracy again is most appropriate.

5. 3.186 inches. A high degree of precision is required and so the answer is given to the nearest 1/1000 inch.

6. 6.85 cm

7. 74.4 km/h   9.   £145.23

8. 36.1°   10. 38.9 m.p.g.

1A

1.	22 052	11.	349
2.	1294	12.	457
3.	1854	13.	7636
4.	103 149	14.	28 746
5.	55 285	15.	666
6.	216	16.	9597
7.	4316	17.	8015
8.	107 532	18.	12 288
9.	441	19.	256 851
10.	2627	20.	3286

1B

1.	£33.35	11.	£3.70
2.	£410.77	12.	£42
3.	£3.20	13.	£0.86
4.	£0.94	14.	£0.07
5.	£4.81	15.	£3.52
6.	£23.89	16.	£63
7.	£2.52	17.	£275.20
8.	£60.48	18.	£57
9.	£2.47	19.	£39.50
10.	£16	20.	£8.40

The exercise requires a good understanding of the notation used for decimal currency.

Watch out for 'silly' answers – a good opportunity to emphasise the importance of estimation and checking.

                    No rounding required

1C [C] Denotes 'Cancel last entry'

1. **a)** (i) [C] 83 =   (ii) 198

    b) (i) 219 + 127 =   (ii) 1203
    c) (i) 39.6 − 36.9 + 18.5 =   (ii) 45.5

    d) (i) [C] 4 × 5 =   (ii) 960

    e) (i) ÷ 8 × 3 × 9 =   (ii) 3240
    f) (i) −9.8 + 0.98 + 10.6 =   (ii) 25.51

2.
A	106.25
B	22.85
C	342.15
D	103.2
E	341.71
F	81.34
G	36.03
H	115.37
GRAND TOTAL	574.45

3.
A	£473.96
B	£406.43
C	£321.89
D	£246.94
E	£206.94
F	£21.44
G	£8.57
H	£812.47
I	£844.13

CHECK   £812.47 + £40.23 − £844.13
                        = £8.57

4. **a)** £33.94
    b) £49.97
    c) £18.99

1D

1. £1.57	6. £18.69	11. £9.68	16. £52.35
2. £3.99	7. £24.60	12. £32.42	17. £1.77
3. £23.83	8. £23.47	13. £5.31	18. £11.73
4. £5.45	9. £300.69	14. £1.64	19. £3.61
5. £37.94	10. £2705.57	15. £19.65	20. £7.99

1E

1. Sector angles are: 163°, 81°, 35°, 58° and 23°
3. Sector angles are: 149°, 124°, 62°, 25°
4. Corresponding measurements in metres are: 4.30, 2.30, 1.37, 0.585
5. **a)** £253.54 **b)** £583.14 **c)** £2155.08 **d)** £3156.56 **e)** £41 542.37
6. The multiples are 8232, 54096, 96726
7. **a)** £38 **b)** £1347 **c)** 735 **d)** £986 **e)** £6192
8. **a)** £183.13 **b)** £198.25 **c)** £216.87 **d)** £208.26 **e)** £253.87
   f) £301.70 **g)** £340.07
9. **a)** £165.90 **b)** £186.27 **c)** £119.67 **d)** £265.29 **e)** £386.17

1F

1. **a)** £2.31 **b)** £46.54 **c)** £299.13 **d)** £559.64 **e)** £1745.50
   f) 19.88 **g)** £116.15
2. 60 dollars

1G

1. 0.625	5. 0.286	9. 0.563	13. 12.833
2. 0.636	6. 0.833	10. 0.739	14. 2.455
3. 0.556	7. 0.667	11. 5.429	15. 1.211
4. 0.333	8. 0.417	12. 16.222	

1H

1. 3.53	5. 4 820 000	9. £7.58	13. 1.62
2. 235	6. 131 000	10. 38.4	14. 70.9
3. 1.98	7. 16.3	11. 6.78	15. 88.3
4. 0.005 51	8. 0.436	12. 0.357	

1I

1. D
2. **a)** 0.9, k = 4.5 cm, l = 10.8 cm **d)** 2, a = 10 cm, b = 26 cm
   b) 0.5, i = 6 cm, j = 6.5 cm **e)** 1.7, e = 20.4 cm, f = 8.5 cm
   c) 1.1, c = 13.2 cm, d = 14.3 cm **f)** 2.6, g = 13 cm, h = 33.8 cm
3. **a)** AB = 10.5 km, AC = 25.2 km, AD = 26.6 km,
   BC = 16.1 km, CD = 11.2 km
   b) 19.6 km **c)** 1:350 000
4. **a)** AB 12 cm 7 mm BC 3 cm 2 mm CD 4 cm 7 mm DE 6 cm 8 mm
   EF 12 cm 4 mm FG 4 cm 9 mm GH 4 cm 4 mm HA 5 cm 1 mm
   b) AB 127 m BC 32 m CD 47 m DE 68 m
   EF 124 m FG 49 m GH 44 m HA 51 m
5. **Note:** The linear scale is 1:50 000, i.e. 1 cm:0.5 km and so corresponding
   areas are in the ratio $(1 \text{ cm})^2:(0.5 \text{ km})^2$
   i.e. $1 \text{ cm}^2:0.25 \text{ km}^2$
   a) 8.5 km **b)** 23 cm **c)** 19.2 cm^2
6. 11.3 m

2A

1. **a)**

KEY	8	+	2	+	3	=
DISPLAY	8	8	2	10	3	13

Previous addition carried out and displayed at this stage.

b)

KEY	8	+	2	×	3	=
DISPLAY	8	8	2	2	3	14

Previous addition not *carried out owing to priority of multiplication.*

c)

KEY	8	+	2	−	3	=
DISPLAY	8	8	2	10	3	7

Previous addition carried out at this stage.

d)

KEY	8	−	3	+	2	=
DISPLAY	8	8	3	5	2	7

Previous subtraction carried out at this stage.

e)

KEY	8	−	2	×	3	=
DISPLAY	8	8	2	2	3	2

Previous subtraction not *carried out owing to priority of multiplication.*

2. a)

KEY	24	−	6	−	2	=
DISPLAY	24	24	6	18	2	16

Previous subtraction carried out at this stage.

b)

KEY	24	−	6	÷	2	=
DISPLAY	24	24	6	6	2	21

Previous subtraction not *carried out owing to priority of division.*

c)

KEY	24	+	6	÷	2	=
DISPLAY	24	24	6	6	2	27

Previous addition not *carried out at this stage owing to priority of division.*

d)

KEY	24	÷	6	×	2	=
DISPLAY	24	24	6	4	2	8

Previous division carried out at this stage.

e)

KEY	24	×	2	÷	6	=
DISPLAY	24	24	2	48	6	8

Previous multiplication carried out at this stage.

The results of this section are intended to demonstrate the following points:

(i) Addition and subtraction are treated with equal priority, i.e. in a calculation involving
addition and subtraction only the operations are carried out in the order in which they are entered.

(ii) In the same way multiplication and division are treated with equal priority.

(iii) Operations of multiplication and division take priority over the operations of addition and subtraction.

The effect of priority is most clearly demonstrated when the key/display tables are positioned as shown.

2B This section illustrates the change of priority caused by the introduction of brackets.

1.

KEY	16	−	(	8	−	2	)	=
DISPLAY	16	16		8	8	2	6	10

In each case once the brackets are opened the expression inside the brackets takes priority and its value is displayed when the brackets are closed.

2.

KEY	5	×	(	7	−	3	)	=
DISPLAY	5	5		7	7	3	4	20

3.

KEY	12	÷	(	9	−	5	)	=
DISPLAY	12	12		9	9	5	4	3

4.

KEY	35	÷	(	4	+	3	)	=
DISPLAY	35	35		4	4	3	7	5

5.

KEY	14	−	3	×	(	7	−	5	)	=
DISPLAY	14	14	3	3		7	7	5	2	8

6.

KEY	35	÷	(	12	−	(	9	−	4	)	)	=
DISPLAY	35	35		12	12		9	9	4	5	7	5

Value of expression contained in the inside pair of brackets.

Value of the complete expression contained in the outside pair of brackets.

The division finally carried out.

2C

1.	5	6.	1	11.	68	16.	679	21.	24
2.	31	7.	4	12.	8	17.	18	22.	47
3.	3	8.	3	13.	14	18.	27	23.	21
4.	4	9.	3	14.	11	19.	35	24.	19
5.	5	10.	38	15.	5	20.	177	25.	52

2D

1.	3.52	3.	6.68	5.	1.01	7.	4.36	9.	2.35
2.	1.25	4.	5.02	6.	2.89	8.	6.30	10.	2.80

2E

1.	−3	7.	2	13.	2	19.	−15	25.	−35
2.	3	8.	9	14.	7	20.	−24	26.	−7
3.	−10	9.	−3	15.	−9	21.	−2	27.	27
4.	−4	10.	−7	16.	−20	22.	−5	28.	−24
5.	0	11.	−8	17.	−18	23.	−2	29.	−2
6.	−99	12.	−3	18.	8	24.	−6	30.	2

2F
1. 1
2. −15
3. 30
4. −4
5. −4
6. 5
7. 10
8. 6
9. −8
10. 8

2G
1. −34.8
2. 45.9
3. 0.391
4. 15.8
5. −0.639
6. 4.76
7. 2.44
8. −0.402
9. −95.4
10. −25.0

2H
1. **a)** 9 **b)** 4.7 **c)** 38 **d)** 0.65 **e)** 131 **f)** 25.5
g) 5.4 **h)** 1 **i)** −4 **j)** −4.8 **k)** −8 **l)** −862.8

Can be found by 2 × answer
subtracting 0.8 from to part (i)
answer to (i)

2. 11.6 3. 34.5
4. **a)** £2184.70 **b)** £128.51
c) No. The mean has been heavily influenced by the two extreme values.
5. 3.5 6. **a)** 524 **b)** 67 **c)** 7.82 47.82
7. 1.39 m 8. 1.60 m

3A
1. 16
2. 49
3. 100
4. 36
5. 64
6. 144
7. 8
8. 3
9. 7
10. 11
11. 13
12. 10
13. 100
14. 50
15. 700
16. 8
17. 125
18. 81
19. 32
20. 512
21. 1 000 000
22. 216
23. 1024
24. 2
25. 3
26. 10
27. 10
28. 3
29. 2
30. 0.5
31. 0.125
32. 0.01
33. 0.0625
34. 16
35. 8
36. 9
37. −0.25
38. 16
39. −100 000
40. −125

3B
1. 76.3
2. 9.92
3. 165
4. 12.6
5. 20.3
6. 0.358
7. 0.307
8. 3.91
9. 0.242
10. 5.41
11. 0.338
12. 1.27
13. 36.5
14. 2480
15. 25.1

3C
1. 19
2. 49
3. 75
4. 20
5. 10
6. 6
7. 24
8. 8.8
9. 0.25
10. 2.75
11. 5.40
12. 88.9
13. 0.0680
14. 5.20
15. 0.0306
16. 232
17. 12.9
18. 0.108
19. 11.2
20. 0.363

3D
1. **a)** 6.86 cm **b)** 8.39 cm
c) 10.2 m **d)** 37.7 km
e) 8.84 m
2. 11.3 cm
3. 10.58 m^2
4. Yes. Length of diagonal of box $=$ 67.0 cm
5. **b)** and **d)** are right-angled

3E
1. 6.32
2. 8.06
3. 9.43
4. 7.21
5. 13.0
6. $\begin{pmatrix} -2 \\ -3 \end{pmatrix}$, 3.61
7. $\begin{pmatrix} 3 \\ -2 \end{pmatrix}$, 3.61
8. $\begin{pmatrix} 2 \\ 4 \end{pmatrix}$, 4.47
9. $\begin{pmatrix} 5 \\ 2 \end{pmatrix}$, 5.39
10. $\begin{pmatrix} -6 \\ -2 \end{pmatrix}$, 6.32

3F
1. **a)** 28.1 **b)** 2.37 **c)** 513 **d)** 0.591
2. **a)** 32.5 **b)** 3.79 **c)** 3020 **d)** 0.478
3. **a)** 26.2 **b)** 1.87 **c)** 211 **d)** 0.657
4. **a)** 437 cm^2 **b)** 598 cm^2 5. **a)** 12 km **b)** 13.4 km

3G
1. **a)** 62.5 **b)** 24 **c)** 184 **d)** 0.61
2. **a)** 156 **b)** 15 **c)** 263 **d)** 0.792
3. **a)** 39.5 **b)** 30.4 **c)** 154 **d)** 0.535
4. 16.3 cm **5.** 14.7 seconds

3H
1. 0.512 **2.** 2.79 **3.** 1.93 **4.** 0.958 **5.** 7.43
6. **a)** (i) 0.707 106 7 (ii) 0.923 879 5 (iii) 0.980 785 2
(iv) 0.995 184 7 (v) 0.318 821 7

4C
1. **a)** 1.26 **b)** 16.6 **c)** 29.1 **6.** 2.08, 10.1
2. **a)** 2.16 **b)** 11.3 **c)** 16.1 **7.** 8.92, 88.6
3. **a)** 3.27 **b)** 60.6 **c)** 16.1 **8. a)** 5.00 **b)** 5.02
4. 8.54, 598 **9. a)** 157 **b)** 6600
5. 0.0667, 0.138 **10. a)** 145 **b)** 600
11. Sequence of approximations is
2.828 427 1, 3.061 467 5, 3.121 445 2, 3.136 548 5, 3.140 331 2,
3.141 277 3, 3.141 513 8, · 3.141 572 9, 3.141 587 7, 3.141 591 4,
3.141 923, 3.141 592 6, 3.141 592 6.

5A
1. 37.5% **6.** 3.59% **11.** 40.5% **16.** 131%
2. 44.4% **7.** 87.0% **12.** 161% **17.** 17.7%
3. 46.7% **8.** 134% **13.** 291% **18.** 31.8%
4. 76.7% **9.** 153% **14.** 68.3% **19.** 50%
5. 43.3% **10.** 124% **15.** 72.6% **20.** 17.0%

5B
1. £12.45 **5.** 3.741 kg **9.** 8870.34 m^2 **13.** £588.38
2. £2.08 **6.** 0.644 kg **10.** £164.86 **14.** £2.32
3. £27.52 **7.** 7.1 cm **11.** £4.86 **15.** £17.21
4. 13.11 m **8.** £90 **12.** £16.04

5C
1. **a)** £9.50, £47.50 **e)** 3.29 litres, 30.69 litres **i)** 10.41 kg, 15.23 kg
b) £7.89, £57.19 **f)** 4.01 cm^3, 51.21 cm^3 **j)** 58.13 m^2, 117.03 m^2
c) 36.98 kg, 122.98 kg **g)** 0.01 volts, 0.27 volts
d) 5.59 m, 62.6 m **h)** £108.69, £196.34
2. **a)** £2.30 **b)** £6.10 **c)** £111.06 **d)** £20.96 **e)** £36.24
f) £100.63 **g)** £250.50 **h)** £1.12 **i)** £4.66 **j)** £883.82
3. **a)** £26.93 **b)** £18.83 **c)** £160.43 **d)** £101.54 **e)** £59.13
f) £5.44 **g)** £11.80 **h)** £20.80 **i)** £3396.88 **j)** £11756.21

5D
1. **a)** £16.25, £48.75 **e)** 158.67 cm^3, 210.33 cm^3 **i)** 36.40 km, 442.60 km
b) £2.20, £16.12 **f)** 1.86 secs, 56.14 secs **j)** 7.83°, 156.97°
c) 1.68 litres, 8.18 litres **g)** 52.05 m, 46.15 m
d) 15.81 kg, 170.19 kg **h)** 7.78 lb, 40.82 lb
2. **a)** £59.98 **b)** £30.36 **c)** £11.92 **d)** £4.64 **e)** £16.10
f) £116.99 **g)** £43.10 **h)** £234.51 **i)** £317.97 **j)** £387.13

5E
Reductions are indicated by a '−' sign.
1. 50.0% **3.** 24.1% **5.** 13.8% **7.** −30.3% **9.** 116%
2. 26.4% **4.** 10.8% **6.** −9.43% **8.** −7.24% **10.** −54.3%
A loss is indicated by a '−' sign.

11. **a)** 14.2% **b)** 12.7% **c)** −19.8% **d)** −26.4% **e)** 197% **f)** −67.5%
12. 4.49% i.e. $\dfrac{3.2 \times 1.8 - 3.15 \times 1.75}{3.15 \times 1.75} \times 100\%$

5F
1. a) £41   b) £86   c) £27.40   d) £18.60   e) £68.80
    f) £117.60   g) £106.20   h) £28.58   i) £362.98   j) £336.10
2. a) 80   b) 20   c) 79   d) 50   e) 151
    f) 193   g) 420   h) 381   i) 85   j) 100
3. a) £9.69   b) £10.64   c) £36.45   d) 0.24   e) £0.13

5G
1. a) 83%   b) 26%   c) 32%   d) 55%   e) 68%
    f) 91%   g) 60%   h) 34%   i) 6%   j) 45%   Average 50%
2. a) 75%   b) 23%   c) 29%   d) 50%   e) 62%
    f) 83%   g) 54%   h) 31%   i) 6%   j) 40%   Average 45%
3. a) 82%   b) 54%   c) 65%   d) 64%   e) 96%
    f) 52%   g) 85%   h) 70%   i) 96%

6B
1. 8300   4. 2 400 000   7. 8.63   10. 0.000 003 6
2. 967   5. 5 700 000   8. 0.472
3. 34.1   6. 2.6   9. 0.000 008 7

6C
Answers given in standard form only.
1. 5.6×10^8 4. 5.72×10^9 7. 2.15×10^{-8} 10. 4.0×10^{-10}
2. 2.73×10^8 5. 1.5×10^{10} 8. 6.6×10^{-11}
3. 5.24×10^9 6. 3.2×10^{-8} 9. 2.0×10^{-8}

6D
1. 2.56×10^{10} 6. 1.53×10^7 11. 1.99×10^{-3} 16. 2.13×10^{-5}
2. 8.72×10^8 7. 8.72×10^7 12. 2.12×10^{-8} 17. 1.99×10^{-5}
3. 5.61×10^{10} 8. -1.60×10^9 13. 2.33×10^{-6} 18. 1.76×10^7
4. 44 700   9. 1.75×10^{-9} 14. 1.46×10^{11} 19. 1.15×10^{-9}
5. 1.35×10^5 10. 3.79×10^{-7} 15. 6.87×10^{-5} 20. 70 200

Note: Some calculators have a key which will convert numbers from floating point to scientific notation and vice versa. It is usually labelled $\boxed{F<\>E}$ but will only operate once the $\boxed{=}$ key has been pressed. The same effect can be achieved on another make of calculator by pressing $\boxed{EE}$ or $\boxed{INV}$ $\boxed{EE}$ as appropriate.

6E
1.126×10^8 km or approximately 280 times the distance from the earth to the moon!

7A
1. 0.5   8. 0.6157   15. 0.4679
2. 0.5   9. 0.9703   16. 1.613
3. 1   10. 0.9397   17. 1.00
4. 1   11. 8.144   18. 573.0
5. 0   12. 0.9573   19. 57 300
6. 1   13. 0.6198   20. Tan 90° is *undefined*. It is *not* true
7. 0   14. 0.6600   to say tan 90° = ∞
                                      (See 7C Questions 9, 10)

7B
1. 21.8°   5. 74.6°   9. 48.7°   13. 60.0°   17. 35.6°
2. 41.8°   6. 38.7°   10. 29.9°   14. 30.0°   18. 56.7°
3. 10.8°   7. 55.2°   11. 67.1°   15. 45.0°   19. 41.9°
4. 40.9°   8. 36.3°   12. 41.6°   16. 42.4°   20. 33.9°

7C
1. 0.8192   5. −3.172   9. −5730   13. 130.9°   17. 118.6°
2. −0.8910   6. −0.3843   10. −5 7300   14. 123.2°   18. 158.8°
3. 0.9898   7. 0.1323   11. 137.2°   15. 140.9°   19. 109.7°
4. −0.3443   8. −0.9603   12. 98.5°   16. 150.3°   20. 171.9°

90

7D

1.	6.82	9.	6.51	17.	21.8	25.	35.4
2.	7.52	10.	2.12	18.	233	26.	9.5 m
3.	31.1	11.	10.4	19.	55.0	27.	180 m
4.	3.01	12.	7.37	20.	6680	28.	2.0 m
5.	36.1	13.	9.22	21.	10.5	29.	a) 9.27 nautical miles
6.	24.4	14.	60.7	22.	20.1		b) 28.5 nautical miles
7.	34.5	15.	34.1	23.	218	30.	77.1 km
8.	0.668	16.	80.2	24.	30.7		

8A All measurements are in metres.

1.

	a)	b)	c)	d)	e)	f)	g)	h)	i)	j)
r					3.2	0.35	4.76	4.14	1.32	24.8
d	17.2	24.2	14.6	29.6				8.27	2.63	49.6
c	54.0	76.0	45.9	93.0	20.1	2.20	29.9			

2.

	a)	b)	c)	d)	e)	f)	g)	h)	i)	j)
r (cm)						36.4	18.2			16.2
$\theta°$								130	34.4	
l (cm)	30.2	40.9	589	82.6	122			33.5	14.2	10.2
A (cm^2)	193	649	36 800	3550	3420	672	693			

3. a) 35.3 cm^2 b) 22.4 cm^2 c) 12.8 cm^2
Note: $35.3 - 22.4 \neq 12.8$, i.e. don't work with rounded values.

8B

1.

	a)	b)	c)	d)	e)	f)	g)	h)	i)	j)
r (m)							4.51	0.392	1.65	0.389
A (m)^2	423	2.22	8.25	38.9	74.2	4160			34.3	1.90
V (m)^3	817	0.310	2.23	22.8	60.1	25 300	385	0.252		

2. a) 1380 cm^3 b) 713 cm^2
3. 1130 cm^2, 3580 cm^3

8C

1.

	a)	b)	c)	d)	e)
S (cm^2)	830	3320	7770	1840	41 700
V (cm^3)	1820	14 600	38 800	5580	18 600

2. a) 2.49 cm b) 77.7 cm^2
3. a) 15.1 cm^2 b) 18100 cm^3

8D 1.

	a)	**b)**	**c)**	**d)**	**e)**
r (cm)					6.07
h (cm)			31.5	15.8	
l (cm)	20.2	25.4			13.8
A (cm²)	1230	879	3490	375	379
V (cm³)	2480	1730	12 700	483	

2. 16 m³

8E 1. **a)** 65.0 m²   **b)** 546 m³   **c)** 5.46 × 10⁵ kg

Sin 90° = 1 and
formula becomes

2. **a)** 12.6 m²   **b)** 20.9 cm²   **c)** 15.9 cm²   **d)** 36.3 m²

$$\text{Area} = \frac{1}{2}ab$$

3. **a)** 14.0 cm²   **b)** 70.1 cm²   **c)** 30.0 cm²

4. **a)** 438 cm³   **b)** 3360 cm³   **c)** 427 m³

A 5, 12, 13 triangle
is right-angled:

5. **a)** 115 cm³   **b)** 24 cm²

$$\text{Area} = \frac{1}{2} \times 5 \times 12 \text{ cm}^2$$

8F 1. **a)** 2   **b)** 0.5   **c)** 0.5   **d)** −4
   e) −1.25   **f)** 0.517   **g)** −0.0610   **h)** −0.583   **i)** 1.26

2. **a)** 7.14 m/s. The graph could represent the progress of a cyclist over a period of 7 seconds. The gradient would then represent his *speed* which is seen to be constant.

   b) −2.73 m/s². The graph could represent the change in speed of a car over a period of 11 seconds. The gradient would then represent the *acceleration* of the car which is constant and negative.

8G 1.

	a)	**b)**	**c)**	**d)**	**e)**	**f)**	**g)**	**h)**
P					333.41			324
R						6.08	8.77	12.6
T								
I	84	62.51	136.05	185.64		32.83	117.61	
A	234	294.01	708.91	797.84	420.93			

8H 1.

	a)	**b)**	**c)**	**d)**	**e)**	**f)**
A	293.87	453.26	582.06	523.96	908.17	21 154.50
I	93.87	103.26	162.06	156.16	335.63	11 394.50

2.

	a)	**b)**	**c)**	**d)**	**e)**	**f)**
P	302.36	401.60	265.97	428.81	650.78	3713.29
I	85.16	111.36	143.26	209.69	165.75	2047.24

Note: Some calculators may give answers which differ by £0.01 from those given in 1(f) and 2(f).

8I
1. a) 5.03   b) 12.4   c) 2.43   d) 17.5   e) 18.5
2. a) $a = 7.71$ $b = 6.68$ b) $e = 21.1$ $f = 22.8$
    c) $g = 4.92$ $h = 4.92$ d) $k = 5.62$ $l = 4.68$
3. a) 19.6°   b) 41.9°   c) 47.2°   d) 38.3°   e) 13.0°
4. a) 39.6°   b) 45.0°   c) 37.8°   d) 40.6°

8J
1. a) 52.1   b) 69.0   c) 561   d) 3.05   e) 19.6
2. a) 5.39   b) 17.0   c) 27.4   d) 18.9   e) 5.00

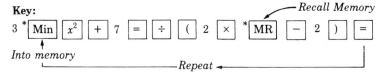

(Cos 90° = 0 and so the cosine rule simplifies to Pythagoras' theorem).

3. a) 34.0°   b) 61.3°   c) 89.6°   d) 143.8°   e) 107.2°
4. a) 55.0°   b) 75.0°   c) 29.0°   d) 138.1°   e) 152.2°

8K
1. $-0.438, -4.56$ 5. $7.41, -0.405$ 9. $-0.5, -3$
2. $-0.459, -6.54$ 6. $8.58, -0.583$ 10. $-0.460, 1.03$
3. $-0.354, -5.65$ 7. $3.83, -1.83$
4. $4.56, 0.438$ 8. $0.633, -2.63$

8L For the quadratic use:

Key:

3 *[Min] [x^2] [+] 7 [=] [÷] [(] 2 [×] *[MR] [−] 2 [)] [=]   *Recall Memory*

↑ *Into memory*

└──────── *Repeat* ◄────────┘

First root
$x_0 = 3$
$x_1 = 4$
$x_2 = 3.8333 \ldots$
$x_3 = 3.828\ 431\ 4$
$x_4 = 3.828\ 427\ 1$

Second root
$x_0 = -2$
$x_1 = -1.833\ 33 \ldots$
$x_2 = -1.828\ 431\ 4$
$x_3 = -1.828\ 427\ 1$

For calculating π:

For initial estimates between 2.0 and 4.3 (approximately) the sequence converges to π. Outside this range the sequence converges to $n\pi$, where n is an integer.

For the circle use:

Key:

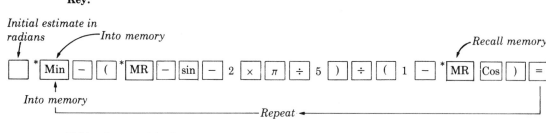

Taking $\theta_0 = 2$ gives $\theta_1 = 2.117\ 173\ 2$, $\theta_2 = 2.113\ 143\ 5$, $\theta_3 = 2.113\ 139$
Angle at centre approx 2.11 rad or 121°. Length of chord in unit circle = 1.74 units.

*Use key appropriate to your calculator. See Section 4A.